FUR COVERED WISDOM

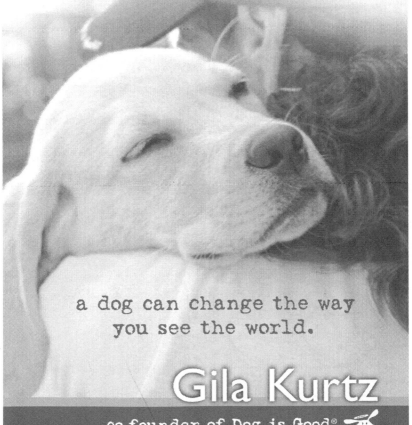

a dog can change the way you see the world.

Gila Kurtz

co-founder of Dog is Good®

Fur Covered Wisdom: A Dog Can Change the Way You See the World

by Gila Kurtz

Cover Design Front by J. Nichole Smith/Steve Myhre
Cover Design Back by Melodye Hunter
Interior Design by Zonoiko Arafat

ISBN: 978-1-944177-02-7 (P)
ISBN: 978-1-944177-03-4 (E)

Crescendo Publishing, LLC
300 Carlsbad Village Drive
Ste. 108A, #443
Carlsbad, California 92008-2999

www.CrescendoPublishing.com
GetPublished@CrescendoPublishing.com

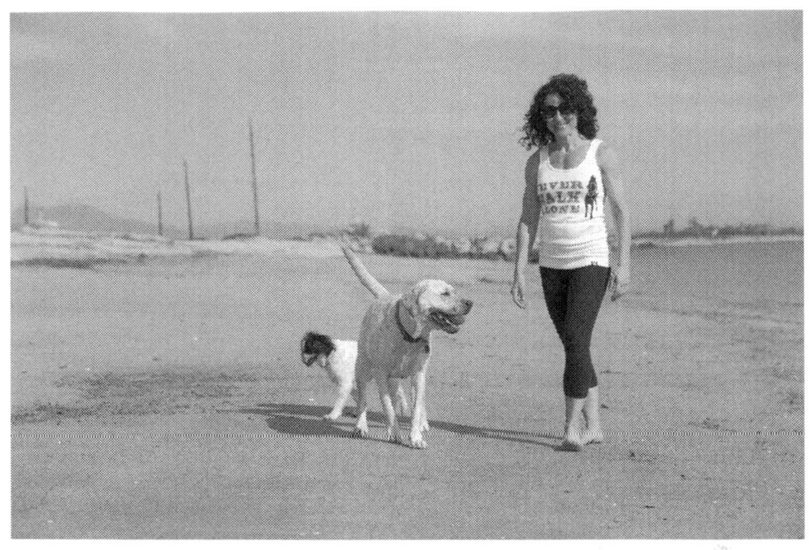

A Message from the Author

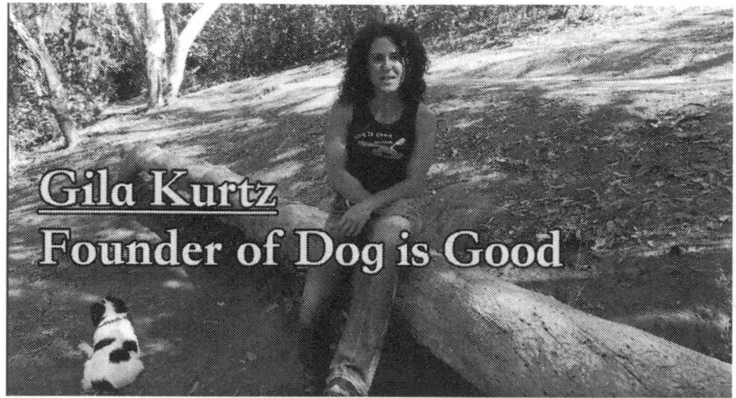

www.dogisgood.com/fur-covered-wisdom

Dog is good is all about celebrating the relationship we have with our dogs and how great they make you feel. My dogs are the inspiration behind the humorous and poignant Dog is Good product line and the commitment I have as a dog trainer to help others maintain lifelong relationships with their dogs.

As a thank you for purchasing *Fur Covered Wisdom,* I would like to gift you 12 e-cards from our award winning greeting card line and access to some of my puppy training videos. Now, you can send a little dose of fur covered wisdom, bring a smile to family and friends, and learn some basic steps to raising a well-mannered, behaviorally sound pup..

With your subscription you will also receive 8 training videos from ***"Your Dog is Good! Training and Coaching at Both Ends of the Leash".***

These videos offer an introduction to training your new puppy. Each 4-5 minute video covers a important component in the training process to raise a well-mannered, behaviorally sound pup including:

- What does success look like when you plan on "de-dogging" your dog?
- Introduction to clicker training and the Attention Cue: helping your puppy become laser focused on you
- Sit
- Down
- Leave it
- Impulse Control
- Stay
- Really Reliable Recall: Perfecting "come when called"

You can access all of these complimentary BONUS GIFTS here:

www.dogisgood.com/fur-covered-wisdom

Love for Fur Covered Wisdom

"I have met some amazing people through my work as a dog behavior expert and Gila Kurtz is no exception. As someone who has also turned a love of dogs into a business, I can relate to Gila's journey. The passion, the hard work that drives you into the ground and the burn-out that forces you to reevaluate your journey and embrace the life you want with the people you want to live it with. Gila's stories will remind everyone that life does not have to be a game of tug of war. The correlation she makes between dog behavior and personal happiness provides easy to apply lessons that we all can use and learn by. If things are moving too fast, you feel overwhelmed and dissatisfied with your life or you just want to make a few changes, take the time to read this book – it will make all the difference."

Victoria Stilwell,
Star of Animal Planet's hit show: It's Me or the Dog, Best selling author, world renowned dog trainer

"Imagine a year-long journey with a dog becoming your new eyes to see the world through? Imagine being visually impaired and having a look through new lenses and being given the opportunity, through your dog, to rediscover your true passion. As we all walk through life sometimes we are blinded to life's beauty and amazing gifts. Through the heart-felt stories shared by Gila Kurtz you will feel connected to your own purpose and passion and realize that you, too, can see the world differently."

Terri Levine,
Best selling author of Coaching is For Everyone

"This book is a total dog – full of fun, love, compassion and wit. Just like my pups, I found myself wanting to cuddle up with it and savor its company, as each chapter is layered in simple, yet profound wisdom and practical applications to all aspects of my life – business, play and personal relationships. As I dug deeper and deeper into the pages, I kept thinking, "I'm gonna give this to my whole family for Christmas – this book SO gets me!" Since finishing the book, I still find myself looking at my own dogs and saying, "Teach me, oh Furball Sensei" as Fur Covered Wisdom made me truly realize just how beautiful their approach to life is. Just don't make the mistake I made when I first started reading this on a long road trip – have a pen and paper ready, because you will find yourself wanting to take notes, underline many of Gila's personal stories that echo your own and "dog-ear" entire pages that you'll want to re-visit later. "

Lorien Clemens,
Director of Marketing- PetHub, Pet Industry Woman of the Year (2014)

Table of Contents

DOG
GOOD

Acknowledgements

Life is a huge puzzle. At the beginning, we don't know how many pieces we have or exactly what the final picture will look like. As we start to put the pieces together, each one representing experiences, people, and even pets in our lives, they seemingly fall into place. At other times, despite searching over and over again, you struggle to find the right one. Then, when you least expect it, the piece you needed magically appears. Over the years, many people have helped me put together my personal puzzle masterpiece.

To my mom: I am grateful for all the sacrifices you made throughout my life to ensure I had everything I needed. Thank you for teaching me the importance of being strong, independent, and committed to achieving my dreams, even in the face of challenges.

To my dad: You left this world too soon but I want to thank you for being an amazing example of living one's truth and for your compassion towards all human beings, for sharing your love of teaching, and for showing me the power of simple acts of kindness.

To my "baby sister" Ronit, thank you for being one of my best friends, for always believing in me, and for embracing my "over-achiever" approach to everything I do.

To my brother Jeremy, thank you for showing me that perseverance through moments of difficulty reveal your true strengths and gifts to the world. You may not realize the impact your personal accomplishments have had on me.

To my lifetime best friend Elizabeth, whom I've known since I was 10 and who knows me better sometimes than I even know myself. Thank you for always being my rock, for your faith in me, and for listening to me whenever I needed you.

To my dearest friend Victoria, thank you for your pragmatic approach to life. I have always looked up to you and admired your personal strength, discipline, humor, and loyalty. Thank you for your selfless friendship, for all the lessons you have taught me, for always having time for me, and for reminding me that life can be whatever you want to make of it.

To the amazing women who surround me daily, Christy, Beke, and Gayle: You lift me up, encourage me, cheer me on, challenge me, and accept me completely for who I am, quirks and all. I could not be where I am today without you. My heart and soul have been touched by your kindness, generosity, and constant support as I strive to reach my personal and professional goals.

To my daughter: my greatest gift, thank you for believing in your mom and for giving me the chance to watch you soar as you pursue your passions and follow your dreams.

To my husband (and business partner) who has the patience of a saint: thank you for all the life experiences you have provided for me, for giving me the chance to open many new doors and walk down different paths over the years, for your integrity and master ability to lead others with ease, and for always choosing to do the right thing. I am grateful for your unwavering support, understanding, and love.

To the precious dogs who have profoundly affected my life, Zoe, Sasha, Henry, and BOLO: thank you for the smiles you bring to my life and for reminding me that there is a treat available for the taking every single day.

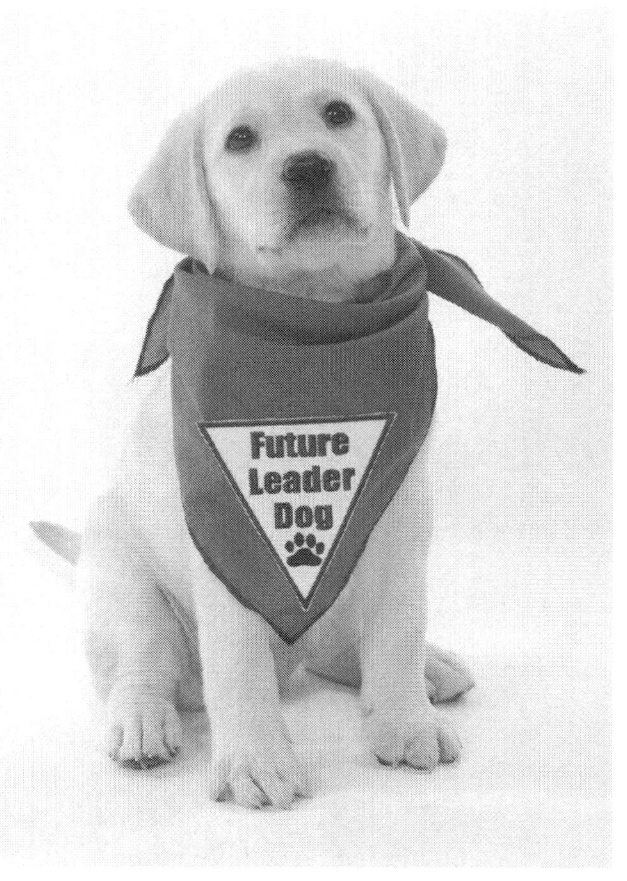
Future
Leader
Dog

Introduction

Automobiles have cruise control to maintain driving speed and ensure you don't have to think about how much or how little pressure is required on the gas pedal. The interesting thing about cruise control is that you are just cruising—there is no variation in the driving experience, which makes it possible for you just to "tune out." A little over a year ago, I was shaken out of "cruise control" by the most adorable Labrador puppy.

Up until her arrival, I was driving down the road of life on cruise control. Each day, I went through the motions, doing everything expected of a supportive wife, nurturing mom, and successful businesswoman. Suddenly, this high-energy puppy pulled me off course, forcing me down a new road—no cruise control allowed.

As someone who fits more in the first six hours of a day (which usually starts at 4:15 am) than most fit in an entire day, it was no surprise to those around me when I decided to add "just one more thing" to my plate. I wanted to dedicate a year of corporate giving through my company, Dog is Good, to an amazing organization: Leader Dogs for the Blind. Because my modus operandi has always been "If it's worth doing, it's worth overdoing," raising funds for the organization was not enough. I thought it would be even better if I combined fundraising efforts with personally raising and training a future Leader Dog puppy. "I figured, I'm already a professional dog trainer, so I can juggle many things at once while having tons of energy... How hard could this be, right?"

The goal: to raise a well-mannered, behaviorally-sound dog who will then go on to provide independence and a life-changing experience to someone blind or visually impaired. And so a seven-week-old pup, who we named BOLO (Be On the Look Out), came into my life. Over the course of our year together, my perfectionist approach to life was greatly challenged, which led to an overwhelming feeling of unhappiness and a pending "burnout" that would shake me to my core.

This book is a year of self-discovery through the eyes of Dog. BOLO came into this world to be the "eyes" for someone visually impaired. Over the course of our year-long journey on this path, she gave me a chance to look at my world through new lenses, providing me with renewed vision; helped me rediscover my true passions and purpose; and gave me hope as I re-evaluated how I was driving down the road of life.

For those who know me, the personal stories may come as a surprise. A master perfectionist, I have always been exceptional at maintaining the image that others perceive. That said, my hope for anyone taking time to read this book is that you will find relatable elements that help you realize that we are not alone in our fears, insecurities, and desire to live life fully and happily.

A dog truly can change how you see the world.

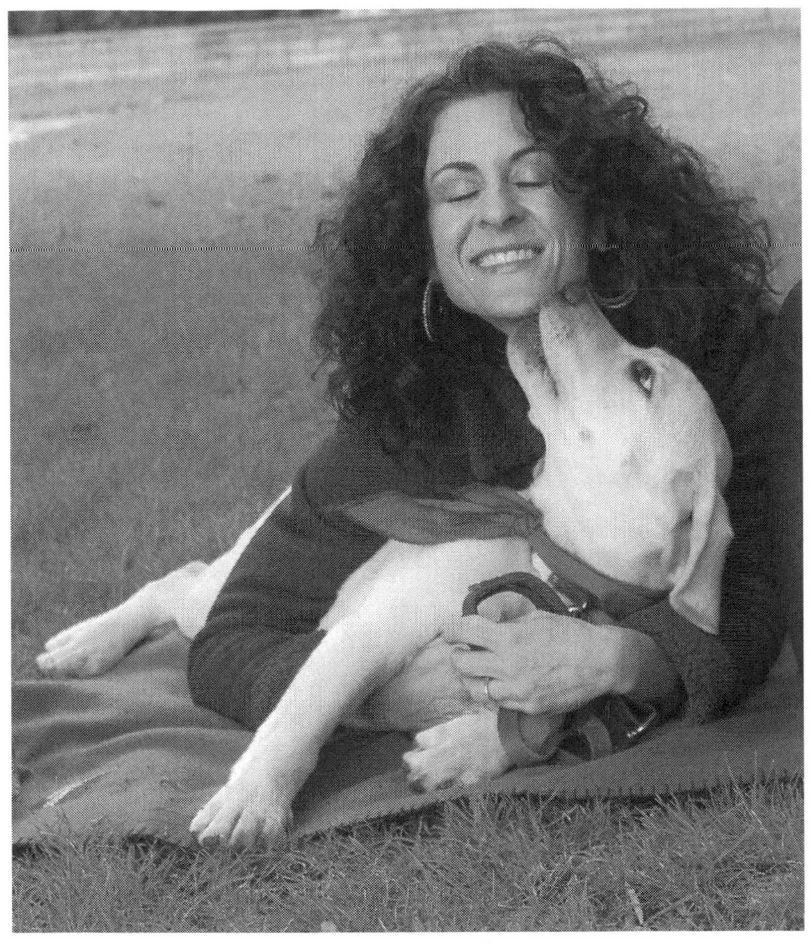

Chapter One

Chase Your Dreams

-1-

Dogs don't hold back. They see something they want and go after it. No matter what obstacles get in the way, the sheer act of chasing becomes the reward in and of itself. In the many years I have worked with dogs, I have observed how they go after what they want, with no hesitation at all. They do not stop to analyze the situation or contemplate the pros and cons. They try different strategies and maintain persistence in the face of challenges. They have a target and go after it, almost always elated in the process of the chase.

In addition to the dogs I have trained professionally over the past 14 years, four very special dogs have been a huge part of my daily life. Zoe was my first dog. A Labrador/Dalmatian mix—who quickly earned the name "Pesto Puppy"— she tested my patience on a daily basis. Sasha, a hound/pointer mix was the second dog to come into our home. Rescued from a shelter, she was sweet, gentle and soulful. Her presence brought a tremendous sense of calm and peace to our home. Henry, a Japanese Chin, was the result of my daughter's relentless persistence, which finally wore her father down. The fourth dog was BOLO, a yellow lab full of life, who was initially supposed to be with us for only a year, during which I would raise, socialize, and train her to become a future Leader Dog for the Blind.

For those of you who have seen dogs dreaming, you know how entertaining that can be. Their entire bodies seem fully engaged in whatever movie is taking place in their head. Of my four dogs, the two that seemed to have the most active dreams were my hunter, Sasha and the very active retriever, BOLO.

BOLO almost never slows down, so it is rare to see her dreaming, but when she does, it seems apparent she is quite intent on getting whatever it is she is chasing. It is possible that she is chasing her favorite ball, but it's more likely she is chasing playful birds at a particular park we frequent. Watching this in action in real life is unbelievably comical. The birds work as a team, diving down in her direction, flying low enough and just in front of her to keep her engaged in this entertaining game.

One of the things I love most about watching BOLO chase after these birds is the look illuminating from her expressive eyes. Her eyebrows are raised, and her mouth is pulled back in a huge smile; her tail is at full tilt and wagging intensely. She stops only briefly and, with her tongue hanging out, seems to want to shout my way, "Do you see what I am doing? Do you see how close I am getting to the birds? Do you see how much fun I am having?" Her tenacity is unbelievable, and it draws the attention of several people in the park who think I have hired these birds to wear her out. It is fascinating to see how she will continue the chase for as long as we are there. In fact, despite *never* catching one of the birds, she continues to go after them with such exuberance that her determination is quite eye-opening. She never once entertains the idea that she might never catch one of those birds. Instead, she goes after them as though she will, has a blast during the pursuit, and never gives up.

I can only assume that as she sleeps, the dreams that fill her head are of these moments chasing the birds at the park. Watching her in the actual chase, I started to wonder about the dreams we create for ourselves. How many people start off chasing their dreams, only to stop when faced with challenges and distractions that pull them off course? At what point do we begin to allow life to just happen to us vs. proactively pursuing it with passion and determination? Do people generate new dreams and change course or do they stop dreaming altogether?

Like many people in their youth, I had big dreams. As life happened around me, those dreams shifted. Major life decisions would present me with new doors of opportunity. Reaching forward to open those doors, I would awaken to new dreams that would take me down different paths. It would not be until later, when dogs entered my life, that I would circle back to discover the missing piece in my life was the initial dream I had as a child. Gaining the courage to chase after this dream again would force me to be introspective, evaluate where I was now and where I wanted to go, and focus on the person I intended to be in my relationships, in my work, and in the contributions I wanted to make in the world around me.

"Forget about the fast lane. If you really want to fly, harness your power to your passion. Honor your calling. Everybody has one. Trust your heart, and success will come to you."

~ Oprah Winfrey

When I was a child, I had a dream about becoming a teacher.

My elementary school was a few blocks away from the local synagogue where my father was the principal for the

Jewish studies and Hebrew school programs. Following a visit to his office where I would dig into his package of Stella Dora assorted cookies, selecting only the white and pink frosted covered ones, I would race down the hall to my classroom. I would set my books on the desk, write my name on the chalkboard, and then sit in the teacher's desk to await the arrival of my students.

I was seven years old, speaking to an imaginary classroom, asking questions and prompting answers to the lesson I was "teaching." I had a piece of chalk in one hand, an eraser in the other, and a clean blackboard just waiting to be filled. I walked around the desks, generously doling out compliments and positive reinforcements to my "students" who were engaged and participating in my class. I looked forward to my pretend play just about every day.

As a seven-year-old, I had no knowledge of the concepts of visualization. I did not play the game with set intentions, nor did I write out specific goals or establish milestones to accomplish. I did not ask anyone their opinions or worry about what they thought. I just played this game of teacher because it was fun, I loved being in front of a classroom, and because I loved "motivating my students" and rewarding them with words of praise and acknowledgement. This game became such a regular part of my after-school routine that I began to dream that I would one day become a teacher, loved by all of her students. The dream stayed with me throughout high school and into college, where I graduated cum laude with a degree in education.

I was lucky—I determined early on what dream to chase. Everything I did along the way brought me closer to my goal and, with it, the ultimate experience of living out my dream as a real high school teacher.

As life happens, circumstances and various events began to pull me in different directions. During my first year teaching, I met the man who became my husband one year later. At the completion of my second year, I married Jon, a military officer who swept me off my feet and whisked me away to embark on my first of 11 moves over a 20-year period. Frequent moves made it challenging to land a teaching position. To adapt, I searched for new dreams to follow and left teaching to pursue more portable career and business opportunities, which I thought would be equally rewarding.

In the ensuing years, I succeeded in growing a profitable lingerie home party business, built a successful sales force for a skin care and wellness company, and owned and operated a thriving gourmet coffee vending business. Seven years into the marriage, I had lived in five different locations. I was making money, but, despite what I was achieving, I did not feel successful and I was not very happy. It was at this time that Zoe entered my life. While we were living in Japan and still childless, I managed to convince Jon to let me adopt a too young, highly energetic Dalmatian/Labrador mix. She joined our family for all of the wrong reasons—but I did not know any better. I knew absolutely nothing about dogs at the time, yet I fell in love the moment I saw her. Her indescribable cuteness combined with my need for something to nurture and care for solidified her addition to our family. At the time, I had no idea that she would ultimately be the catalyst that would send my life in a completely new direction.

Upon leaving Japan, Jon was assigned a job at the Pentagon, so we moved to Northern Virginia. We had been back in the states for a couple years when I had an epiphany. This occurred one afternoon at the local dog park and would be the first of many in the years to come.

Zoe earned the nickname "Pesto Puppy" (because she was relentless in her quest for attention) and basically controlled the house and all outings. She was in usual form one day at the park, having "trained" me quite well to pick up tennis balls wherever she dropped them. She was only part retriever of course, so how could I possibly expect her to bring the ball back to me? When I picked up the ball to throw it back into play, I noticed a gentleman walking into the dog park with six dogs. I said hello and commented that his house must be crazy with so many dogs. He laughed and told me that they were not his dogs. This was his third time to the park that day, and each time he brought an entirely different pack. He told me that he would collect the dogs from people's homes and bring them out to walk and play. "You just play with dogs all day?" I asked. "Yep," he replied with a huge smile on his face.

This guy got to play with dogs from eight am until six pm at night. There were occasions where he had dogs late into the evening and on weekends if a family was out of town. He was having the time of his life, and he was getting PAID for it. He was a professional dog walker, and he was earning six figures doing it. What?! Are you kidding me?! This was a complete anomaly to me, but I instantly wanted in. I called Jon right at that moment to tell him that when we made our next move to Florida I was going to become a professional dog walker.

When we arrived in Panama City Beach, Florida later that year, I discovered a minor problem that would put an immediate halt in my attempt to become a highly paid dog walker. Apparently rural Panama City Beach did not have the same needs for in-home dog care as metropolitan Washington D.C. In this part of Florida, people were not away from their homes for more than twelve hours a day. Many just let their dogs roam in rural areas or kept them tethered outside. At this point, I was hooked on the idea of working with dogs. I thought it through and came to the conclusion that I should combine my growing love for dogs with my passion for teaching people. My dream switched from dog walker to dog trainer. Considering I did not know how to train my own unruly and highly demanding Dalmatian, this would be an adventure, but it would be an adventure that would reunite me with my original dream. I was going to be a teacher again.

My new involvement in the world of dogs would ultimately bring the three other canines into our home and lives. With every new dog and every move, I was presented with new opportunities. My dog training business was thriving, and my focus on the positive effects of the dog-human relationship brought me to a place where I could create a vision for another dog-related business.

Dog is Good, a lifestyle brand for dog lovers, was born out of my love for dogs and the desire to convey, through a variety of products and messaging, how great I felt in the presence of dogs. Initially it was easy to combine both dreams: helping people train their dogs and grow a dog-themed business from the ground up. I was able to balance an active dog training business while learning about product development, manufacturing, sales, and marketing.

Then something exciting happened: Dog is Good started to rapidly grow. With this new company taking off, my availability for dog training became incredibly limited. Over an eight-year period, my life would become fully consumed by my ambition to grow this business. A perfectionist by nature, I did not want to admit things were spiraling out of control. I continued to pursue my dream with a fury until a Yellow Lab would force me to stop long enough to look in the mirror and begin my search for the woman I could recognize again. It would be the beginning of a two-year journey taking me back to my seven-year-old self. When there is intense passion to chase after a dream, the dream becomes the fuel that ultimately gives life the meaning we search for.

"Twenty years from now you will be more disappointed by the things that you didn't do than by the ones you did do. So throw off the bowlines. Sail away from the safe harbor. Catch the trade winds in your sails. Explore. Dream. Discover."

~ Mark Twain

- Dreams evolve over our lifetime. At any point you can go after new dreams or revisit old ones. Just remember never to stop dreaming. You are NEVER too old to chase them, and if you are willing to do whatever it takes during the chase, an amazing journey will unfold before you.

- Dream big: "It doesn't take any more energy to create a big dream than it does to create a little one," said General Wesley Clark. What do you really want? What do you love to do? What are your unique talents and personal qualities? When you get to where you want to go, what does your life look like in five, ten, twenty-five years?

- Do not limit your dream based on what your internal voice believes is possible. Dream as though ANYTHING is possible. "When you cease to dream, you cease to live," said Malcolm Forbes.

- Take action and stop being afraid. We let fear cheat us of the life we deserve: Fear of failure, fear of the unknown, and fear of what others will think paralyze us and lead to regret. Fear provides validation in excuses:" I will pursue my dream once my child is out of school, when I lose weight, when I get my degree, when I get a promotion, when I get out of debt, when the economy improves, when my husband retires, etc."

- Quit worrying about what everyone else will think. No one gets to wake up in your head each day and feel your personal joy, sadness, pride in accomplishments, or frustrations with failures. They don't get to be you and really don't spend much time thinking about what is going on with you. Get out of your own way and chase what you want with blinders on.

Chapter Two

Keep Your Eye on the Ball

-2-

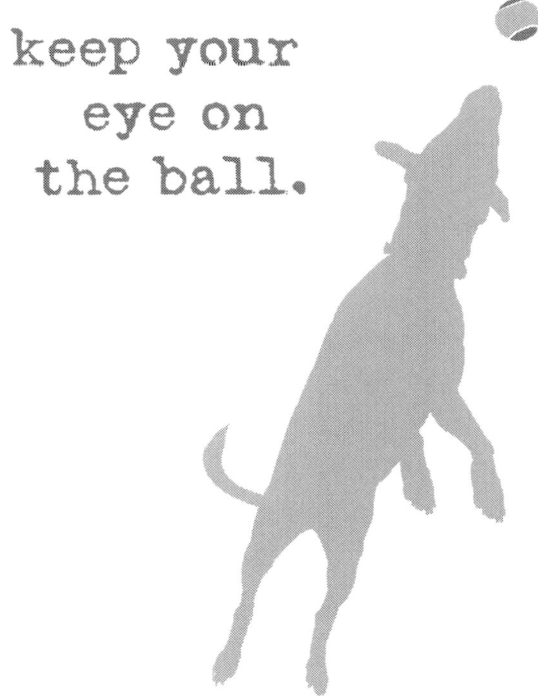
keep your
eye on
the ball.

You know you have a ball-obsessed dog when the moment the ball comes out everything else in the world ceases to exist.

Of the four dogs in my life, two were ball-obsessed (Zoe and BOLO). One was rabbit-, squirrel-, and duck-obsessed (Sasha), and the fourth really could not care less—he's basically a cat in a dog's body (Henry).

During our time living in the state of Washington, Jon and I frequently took Zoe on walks to a large open field. The perimeter of the area was lined with tall grass, home to countless foul balls. The moment we let her off her leash, her nose hit the ground and she would start to pace back and forth along the edge of the grass. At a certain point, she would stop and look toward the grass as if she was making a final calculation before diving into the thick of it. Sure enough, once she momentarily disappeared, she would pop back out with a baseball in her mouth. I swear, she could literally smell "round." The moment we threw that ball, she would become fully engaged and focused on it. Only part retriever, she was consistent in the chase, but she never quite mastered the "retrieve" part of the game. She always stopped halfway on the return and dropped the ball, forcing me and Jon to walk to wherever it was. Very often, while racing toward a thrown ball, she would suddenly make a sharp turn, following some random scent. Sometimes she would re-engage and go to the ball, but most of the time Jon and I were relegated to completing both the toss and retrieve portions of the fetch game.

In contrast to Zoe, the instant BOLO sees a ball, the rest of the world fades immediately into the background. Whether it's at the dog park, the beach, the hiking trails, the house, or the office, when BOLO sees a ball, she is laser-focused. Racing after her ball is the highlight of her day, and she will stay glued on it, oblivious to the distractions around her, until we tire and put the ball away.

The two dogs were very interested in balls, but each had completely different approaches. Zoe never really fully engaged in the game of fetch. She would pursue the ball with interest initially but always got "pulled off course," and even when she played, she would initially chase the ball with intensity but never follow through with the game. She always left things hanging. On the other hand, BOLO won't take her eye off the prize and will race after it like a horse in the Kentucky Derby until we stop the game.

To be everywhere is to be nowhere."

~ Seneca

Following high school, it was pretty easy for me to focus on what I wanted to do. Making a decision at 18 about your entire future is a tall order, but I was fortunate in that I knew early on exactly what I wanted to pursue and was laser-focused throughout both high school and college. People who know me personally understand that I have moments where I can be a bit obsessive. Okay, that might be an understatement—nonetheless, I found myself in high school and college noting qualities and skills of teachers who I thought were outstanding. I wanted to emulate the best of the best as I worked through my education degree to become the kind of teacher that not only taught information but also had a positive, lasting impact on her students. Following college graduation, I did just that. At the time, there were no distractions. It was easy to stay focused doing something I loved.

Fast forward to marriage into the military and a new reality that meant I would no longer remain in the same home for any length of time. The wonderful thing about life as a Navy wife was that I was largely guaranteed to live in lovely coastal towns. The downside was that just as I would find my way, I had to move. When you are in love, you welcome new adventure, and so that is what I did. My intense determination to be successful kept me focused on the new can of balls I would have to open in each new location. Yet, just as I would gain traction in a new venture, another move would show up on the horizon. I would find myself like Zoe: pulled off the chase to pack up, follow something new, and reinvent myself once again in a new location.

While I happily supported my husband as he soared successfully through the military ranks—I was a pretty darn good Navy wife—I found myself feeling a bit unaccomplished. Don't get me wrong, I was and still am incredibly proud of the amazing leader Jon became throughout his stellar naval career, but with each move my focus became a bit fuzzy. I no longer had my eye on the prize of teaching and would turn my attention to whatever I could do wherever we were stationed. If it was selling lingerie in home parties, I was laser focused on meeting people and enticing them to host parties in their homes. If it was waitressing, I was focused on being efficient, affable, and customer-centered. If it was building a sales force of independent reps, I was focused on recruiting and training. If it was teaching baking classes to Japanese women when we lived in Japan, I was focused on creating the most entertaining baking sessions. If it was operating my own gourmet coffee vending business, I was focused on finding ideal locations and providing the best service in town. When I became a mom, I was focused entirely on the care and nurturing of this little human being. As you might guess, there were an awful lot of balls thrown my way. With the exception of bringing my daughter into the world, there were none that I was going after with zest. Moving constantly made it difficult, and I became keenly aware that something was missing inside. I felt no intrinsic sense of joy and could not summon the enthusiasm that is present when you are doing something you are passionate about.

One day, and completely unexpected, a new ball was tossed into the game. It was the chance meeting of a professional dog walker who introduced to me a completely new world of opportunity. I look back and am reminded that, had it not been for Zoe and her need to get to the park to play, this encounter would have never happened, and I would likely be in a completely different place in my life right now. The decision to pursue a career as a professional dog trainer gave me a renewed sense of direction and, for the first time in years, I felt excitement and enthusiasm as I went through the coursework and apprenticeship to become a certified professional dog trainer.

My interest in dog behavior and the joy I received when working with dogs and their owners brought clarity into my life. When you don't have clarity on your life's purpose, it becomes incredibly challenging to keep your eye on the ball. Combining my focus and drive helped to quickly grow a successful dog training business. Things were better than ever: I was teaching and now had a portable career that I could take with me no matter how many times the Navy asked us to move. For the first time in 11 years, I felt like I had a purpose again.

Although I did not realize it at the time, opening my life and heart to the world of dogs would ultimately send me on a journey of self-discovery. My dogs were changing me and how I lived each day. This change spawned another ball: Dog is Good. The idea to develop a line of products that gave people an opportunity to express their love of dogs, share with the world who they were as a dog lover, and celebrate the positive benefits of the dog-human bond would begin to capture more and more of my attention. With another move pending came the preparations for a fourth re-launch of my dog training business and the initial launch of Dog is Good, a lifestyle brand for dog lovers, inspired by Dog.

I had not been this excited in years. Splitting my time between dog training and building this new business was going to be awesome! How could it be any less than exhilarating when I got to combine my love for dogs with the creation of fun and meaningful products... *and* get to do this with my husband?

I was incredibly confident that I could effectively keep my eye on both balls with ease. In the beginning, it WAS easy, but then Dog is Good started to grow. It grew fast and, at every turn, began to generate more balls.

This fast rate of growth began to tax my ability to keep my eye on all the balls. It was as though one of those tennis ball machines was placed in front of me every day, shooting ball after ball directly at me. This machine was propped up at the start of my day (4:15 am) and remained operable until late in the evening. As a small business owner, I knew I needed to hit as many of those balls as possible. By mid-day, I was operating on overdrive and hoped no one could detect the mayhem that was taking place inside my head. Dog is Good was experiencing significant growth year over year and, with every successful milestone, it seemed as though the speed of that tennis ball machine was increased. More balls were coming at me faster than ever before, and they were not exclusively Dog is Good. Other balls representing family commitments, social obligations, volunteer work, time for friends, dog training, and running errands or doing chores were also popping out of the machine.

One afternoon at the dog park, as I played fetch with BOLO, I noticed that despite the numerous other balls being thrown or available on the ground throughout the park, she was solely focused on the one ball we were playing with. Every time she trotted back in my direction, she was thrilled with herself. She was having a blast. It became clear that BOLO's focus made it possible for her to enjoy the game. She wasn't multitasking or constantly switching which ball she would go after, and she certainly wasn't stressing over things that happened earlier in the day or anxious over what might happen tomorrow. She was in pure bliss and I wanted that bliss back in my life.

"Never confuse motion with action."

~ Benjamin Franklin

My days were filled with activity as I became buried working in my business rather than on my business. I realized I had to stop attending to every single ball flying toward me. At this point, I was just a standing target, letting things get thrown at me, and I was losing myself quickly in the process. It was time to turn off the machine so I could recalibrate my personal GPS and get focused on what I really wanted.

The only way to begin this process was to put my trust in the hands of capable people who were ready to go after balls that represented their area of expertise. With a vast reduction in balls shooting at me from all directions, my brain could now re-evaluate which balls I would lock in on as my target. My assignment would be to select only the most important balls that would help me reach my goal and find a way to enjoy it in the process.

The task seemed easy enough, yet all I could do was sit in my chair with a blank look on my face. The only thoughts running through my brain were the random reminders about what was on my current mile-long list of things to do at work and at home. There still seemed to be too many balls to juggle. I became frustrated because I knew I did not want my life to look the same five years later as it did now, but I had no clue what I *really* wanted. I had forgotten why I was trying to focus on any balls and could not pick out the ones that held my true passions.

I sat for a very long time before a few images and ideas started to form. I was inspired by these thoughts and began focusing more and more on what was taking shape. A self-proclaimed master of multitasking, the first thing I came to terms with was that this approach made me a master of nothing. In order to begin a new focused approach to each day, I made a commitment to concentrate on one, and only one, very important "ball" each morning: **ME**.

"The shorter way to do many things is to do only one thing at a time."

~ Mozart

The turning point came on December 27, 2014 when I made a conscious promise to myself that I would no longer start my day by opening my email and starting to work. This was a practice I had engaged in my entire working life (well, at least since email became an integral part of communication). Instead I would use my quiet morning time to focus on rediscovering my passions and create better short-term, as well as long-term, goals.

Just as I kept my body fit and strong through exercise, I would now keep my mind healthy and positive through reading, goal setting, and visualization.

To help me identify only those balls that would help me achieve my business/career, personal, and financial goals, I had to get very specific and clear on what I wanted. I had to put a timeline on when they would be achieved. I had to have a way to measure my progress and be able to identify when I actually got there. In essence, I had to fully envision what success looked like to me, and then work backwards to put it all together.

Anything that did not align with my goals was deemed a distraction, which is what pulls you off course while giving you the illusion that you are moving forward. Intent on not falling victim to the "squirrel syndrome," I identified all the "shiny objects" and began to put systems in place that would keep me on track. With this clear vision and goals, I could now keep my eye on the ball just like BOLO.

To gain better focus:

- Decide what success looks like to you. Gain clarity by establishing detailed written goals. Identify the top three things that will get you closer to your goal, write them down, and put them in front of you. Everything else is a distraction.

- Identify those things that pull you off course. Are you obsessed with digital data? Set a specific time every day when you will attend to your social media; otherwise, turn those apps and notifications off.

- Clear the clutter from your home, office, and daily routine. The piles of paper on your desk, the trail of "stuff" throughout your home, and over-scheduling your days create significant distractions. Set aside one day a week to tackle each of these areas and maintain upkeep on a weekly basis.

- Understand your personal routine and set boundaries for others. Identify the most productive part of your day and give people a time frame to limit interruptions. Turn off your phone during this time as well.

Chapter Three

Never Walk Alone

-3-

When you have dogs, you walk every day... or at least you should be walking every day. With the many places the Navy took us over the years came several opportunities to create memories on walks in a number of beautiful places. As much as I love walking with my friends, my walks alone with the dogs are different. They are the only moments when my mind seems to slow down and a sense of calm takes over my harried day.

A few months after bringing Zoe into our lives, she and I would bond over morning hikes. A short walk from our home on the military installation in Japan was the base of Mt. Yumihari. I looked forward to the trek up to the top with my energetic and curious puppy. Whether we took shortcuts up the side or spent time on the winding road leading to the peak, every walk was an adventure. Once at the top, with a now-tired puppy, I would delight in the serene beauty that lay before me. There would be people around me involved in Tai Chi and others taking pictures. I would just sit there quietly and watch the sunlight dance on the water in Sasebo Bay or marvel at the huge naval ships as they navigated the islands. It was simply breathtaking.

Zoe was six months old when we returned to the states and, now pregnant with my daughter Abby, she was my daily walking buddy. As my body changed, Zoe seemed to sense that a change in her life was imminent. Our beautiful daughter arrived in October and now dictated when Zoe and I would head out on walks. With baby in tow, I thought it would be better for Zoe to walk in areas where she could be off her leash. She was thrilled, but I quickly learned the headaches of dealing with a dog who will not come when called. Whether it was on a walk or at a park, Zoe would teach me patience and great restraint.

With the addition of Sasha a few years later, daily walks became much more relaxing.

Because our walks together took place early in the morning and later in the evening, I was fortunate to witness some of the most glorious sunrises and sunsets just about every day. Yet it would be our move to Washington State that would provide the most memorable walks of all.

Every day, after dropping Abby off at school, the dogs and I would head for the hills. Miles and miles of trails awaited us. The area was well known for hiking, mountain biking, horseback riding, and—of course—dog walking. I loved this time alone with the dogs. They would delight in the freedom of running off leash to chase rabbits or the occasional deer and then return by my side in complete euphoria. I loved the solitude and the opportunity to let my mind relax. These walks were probably the only walks I have taken where I was truly mindful of my surroundings and how peaceful that made me feel. It was on these trails that I would experience something amazing and surreal. The day was a gloriously sunny day, unusual for the Northwest at that time of year. After about an hour of hiking, I was at the top of a major trailhead. The sky was crystal clear and the brightest blue I had ever seen; the air was fresh and temperate at about 55 degrees Fahrenheit. I stood there taking in the beauty around me. The dogs also stopped as if they realized I was "onto something." Or maybe they just sensed that they needed to stay still so as not to disrupt this perfect moment. Miles away I could see Mt. Baker, snow-capped and glistening in full view. Also a great distance away was Mt. Rainier, the most majestic mountain I have ever seen. I alternated between the two sites in complete awe of nature.

I felt the moment could not get any better until right before my eyes a huge bald eagle flew into sight and settled down on a dead tree trunk. My first thought was, "Great, Sasha is going to go after our national bird and ruin the entire moment." Miraculously she did not. Maybe it was because the eagle was enormous and unlike any bird she had never seen. Both dogs stood there with me quietly. At that moment I remember thinking how grateful I was to be alive, to be with my dogs, and to be standing in that very place at that very moment to witness the quiet beauty that had unfolded in front of me. I felt a keen sense of happiness.

During the years we spent in Washington, I loved my lifestyle. My dog-training business flourished quickly, I had time to enjoy things that were meaningful to me, and I was able to spend time volunteering in my daughter's classrooms. I had successfully adapted to this breathtaking location but, having grown accustomed to the inevitable moves, never quite allowed myself to get fully attached. Our time in Washington ended before I was ready to leave.

Fast forward a couple years to my life in California and the rapid changes that took place. The need to surround myself with the right people became critical to professional development and lifesaving for my personal state of mind.

"Surround yourself with people who make you happy. People who make you laugh, who help you when you're in need. People who genuinely care. They are the ones worth keeping in your life. Everyone else is just passing through."

~ Karl Marx

"Surround yourself with the dreamers and the doers, the believers and thinkers, but most of all, surround yourself with those who see the greatness within you, even when you don't see it yourself."

~Edmund Lee

"It's not where you walk, it's who walks with you." The people you choose to walk by your side can have a profound effect on the paths you take and the experiences you have during this journey called life. When you travel alone on this path, it too will affect who you become and the success you achieve.

My business was gaining momentum like a snowball racing down a hill. It was growing faster than I could keep up. It was very exciting, but my inclination to work like mad turned into a serious workaholic habit. Despite being surrounded all day with amazing people, I spent much of my time alone working on my own projects. A move to a much larger office space finally provided me with the privacy I needed but now isolated me a bit from the rest of the team. With each passing month, I stopped growing my knowledge base and finding inspiration through mentors or like-minded entrepreneurs. I also found myself spending less and less time with friends. When it came to my daughter, the only saving grace to alleviate my "working mommy guilt" was the fact that her show choir took up quite a bit of her time outside of school.

I knew intuitively that, in order to grow both personally and professionally, I had to stop "walking alone" in business and in life. Knowing and doing are two different things, and over an 18-month period, I stagnated personally, lost my enthusiasm, and found myself increasingly lonely and often quite angry. My stress level continued to skyrocket until I woke up one morning and decided to be proactive in inviting the right people to walk by my side. I needed positive and supportive people to influence my attitude, provide guidance with my business decisions, jump-start my social life, and lift me up out the crevice I had fallen in.

The good news is that I already had so many of the right people in my life; the bad news was that my workaholic lifestyle left very little room for anyone. At work, the only way my team could walk with me was if I lifted the self-imposed grip I had on everything. I already had brilliant people, experts in their respective areas of operation, who were just waiting to be unleashed to work their magic. As I allowed myself to truly embrace the trust and belief I had in these people, I began to feel some relief.

Years ago, I frequented lots of networking events, business conferences, and personal development programs. I am not sure where along the way I actually stopped doing this, but I was perceptive enough to know that I needed to get back to this practice. Continued success in my growing company would become dependent on furthering my education and meeting the right people. I sought individuals who had achieved a level of success that I wanted to attain, were in similar stages of growth in their own companies, or were just badass, positive people. I jumped back into the arena to seek out these individuals and, as more people started to walk by my side, I felt rejuvenated. Finding the right mentors does not only aid in guidance, but they also provide tremendous opportunities to learn from both their achievements and failures. Networking with other entrepreneurs who were at similar milestones in their business became a wonderful resource. It was very helpful to exchange ideas and become sounding boards for each other. Lastly, it goes without saying, hanging out with badass, positive people was exactly what the doctor ordered. I can't think of anything more energizing than being around motivated, like-minded, driven, and inspiring people.

On a personal level, I set a goal to spend more time with friends. Yes, I know the fact that I actually had to set a goal to spend more time with friends sounds horrible, but if I didn't, I would get sucked back into the abyss of work. I am blessed with the most amazing friends one could ever ask for. They truly are the most inspiring, caring, giving, thoughtful, empathetic, non-judgmental women I have ever known. I strive to emulate the amazing qualities I find in each of them and, whether they live near or far, I am always uplifted from conversations or time spent together. It became imperative for my sanity to "rejoin them on walks" as often as possible.

"You are the average of the five people you spend the most time with."

~ Jim Rohm

As a parent, we monitor whom our children hang out with. Why? Because we don't want them hanging out with people who will inflict a bad influence on them. Adulthood is no different. To achieve success in life, you need to walk with positive, supportive, goal-oriented, successful people. Conversely, you need to steer clear from poisonous people who will drain you with their complaints, gossip, excuses, and overall negativity toward life.

Life's journey is not meant to be taken alone. Whom you choose to walk with you can make the difference between success or mediocrity, happiness or regret.

- Develop a mindset that attracts successful, uplifting, goal oriented, focused, supportive, and positive people. Remember that these people do not want to surround themselves with others who drain their energy with negative attitudes.

Begin thinking and behaving like the people you want in your circle of influence.

- Expand your associations through organizations and networking groups. As you meet like-minded individuals, foster new relationships by focusing on how you can bring value to them.

- Find a mentor. Learning from someone with experience helps to shorten the learning curve.

- Surround yourself with individuals who treat everyone with respect. You can learn quite a bit about someone based on how they speak to others. Anyone who is rude, makes disparaging remarks, becomes easily agitated, or gossips, or is poisonous.

- Further your growth with a balance of people who encourage and support you in your pursuit of your dreams by challenging you and providing different perspectives. Being around only those who always agree with you will limit how quickly you make progress toward your goals.

- Bring laughter into your life by making sure you surround yourself with people who boost your sense of humor. Maintain and nurture familial relationships and take care of your friendships by staying connected.

As you pursue the best that life has to offer, remember: It's not where you walk, it's who walks with you along the way.

Chapter Four

Make Time for Play

-4-

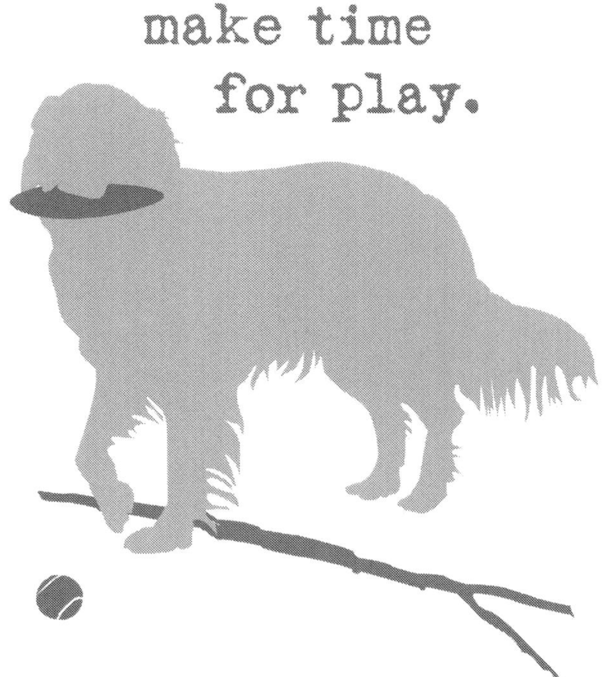

Why do so many people say they want to return in their second life as their dog? It's because a dog's life is so simple. They eat, sleep, play, and repeat throughout the day, every day.

When I travel for business, I have to leave my dogs behind. Hours spent at trade shows do not make for a fun vacation for the pups, so I make arrangements for care that guarantees fun for both dogs. Henry and BOLO have two very distinct temperaments. Henry is a piece of cake to watch. He is mellow, quiet, and not demanding. He is basically a cat. BOLO, on the other hand, is a completely different story. The moment she opens her puppy eyes she is on the go, rarely stopping until those final moments at night when she has concluded there's nothing left to investigate or experience. Everyone loves and enjoys watching Henry. They also love BOLO but are thankful I put her in daycare.

BOLO goes to an awesome daycare and boarding facility, the Ritz Carlton of doggie daycare centers. In addition to a lovely indoor setting, the backyard offers a huge area for running and playing. The trees provide shade and the big dog-bone-shaped pool is the perfect cooling zone, a favorite among all the water dogs. Needless to say, there is plenty of play going on here. One of the benefits many doggie daycares offer is the opportunity to watch your dog on the webcam. This is fantastic unless you find yourself obsessed with watching your dog play. After a long day at a tradeshow, I find myself glued to that webcam. My hope is to catch a glimpse of BOLO as she races past the webcam. It's interesting to watch. Most dogs take any opportunity to play, inviting each other with their play bows and then taking off in a game of chase. Fascinating! Given the opportunity, dogs will play for hours, stopping only to rest long enough to recover and get back in the game. I definitely wish I was more like a dog in this regard.

At home, although I rarely seem to make time for play in my personal life, I always ensure that both Henry and BOLO get to enjoy their playtime. It is interesting to observe how excited and energized they become in anticipation of a trip to the beach, park, or hiking trails. Their entire demeanors change. On the rare occasion when we just can't do more than a quick walk around the block, I notice the difference in their behavior as well. Henry appears less energized and almost "depressed" by mid-day, and BOLO becomes mischievous, getting into anything she can to channel her energy and curiosity. Play is something both dogs and kids do naturally. As puppies grow into mature dogs, they continue to seek out opportunities to play every day. This is what they live for: Eat, play, sleep, repeat. However, as kids grow up, play tends to become less integrated into daily life.

"If one insisted always on being serious, and never allowed him or herself a bit of fun and relaxation, one would go mad or become unstable without knowing it."

~ Herodotus

You got to play! The proverb "all work and no play make Jack a dull boy" could not be more true today for me personally, and likely for countless others. Technology has increased our efficiency but has added distraction and complexity to daily life by making it possible to stay attached to one's work 24/7. With smart phones, laptops, and iPads as our lifelines, we can set up an "office" at any place of business that offers free WiFi. In the event that WiFi may not be available, we have our personal WiFi devices to ensure access to the Internet. Every spare minute is spent doing something digitally. If we discover an unoccupied moment during our day, we immediately pull out the cell phone.

I had most definitely fallen into the trap of constant connectivity. Pathetically, I will admit feeling panicked when I discover no WiFi on a plane traveling across the country, and I shamelessly once stood frozen in the middle of an open meadow while visiting Yosemite Park to preserve the one bar on my cell that would link me back to the office.

Plugged only into work without a plan for play is costly. This is where I found myself. I had become aware that play and laughter were no longer apparent in my life, but I felt stuck and unable to break the vicious cycle that I had created. Not only was I suffering inside, but I also could see where lack of play was negatively affecting my work and my relationships with family, friends, co-workers, and at times, even my dogs. I knew I needed to play more and find ways just to have some good old fun. Unfortunately, somewhere along the way I had forgotten how.

Once fully engaged in every aspect of growing my business, anything that did not seem to support its growth seemed of little importance. At a slow and steady pace, my life was becoming void of fun. With my mind only on building my business, I wasn't aware that "fun" had slipped away. I simply became too focused on business goals and too busy to notice. Then I received a gut-wrenching hit to the stomach while working with one of my dearest friends at a Dog is Good event.

We had set up a Dog is Good boutique booth as vendors for an upscale holiday boutique bazaar. I felt inspired and enthused as I watched the reactions and listened to the responses to the product line as women frantically did their holiday shopping. During a brief lull, I asked my friend what she had planned for the weekend ahead. She began to run down a list of things that included a ride on a party bus with friends on one night and tickets to a concert on another. I was genuinely excited for her and then blurted my thoughts out loud: "Wow, you always have so much fun! I need to add a little fun into my life." It was a casual comment not intended for deep conversation, but her reply to me proved to be the catalyst that would force me to take a long hard look at what was happening to my life. Her response back to me was, "Yeah, I would not want your life for anything—your life is no fun." Her comment was not intended to hurt me, but it stung... it stung really hard. I remained quiet on the topic for the remainder of the evening, but it had ripped open a wound deeply buried inside of me. I knew exactly what she meant. I just did not want to admit it, and suddenly I could not hold back the gushing of emotion that would send me on a downward spiral in the months to follow.

The compulsion to stay plugged in and do everything required to grow my business was generating a brutal stress. It became increasingly harder to laugh, leaving me completely unmotivated to do anything outside of work. It was painfully clear that I was missing the point of living. I was losing weight, something I could not afford to do, and I found myself crying uncontrollably at random moments throughout the day. The energy it took to keep up a positive, enthusiastic appearance that radiated joy and success was leaving me depressed, angry, frustrated, and probably unpleasant to be around. The more I tried to cover things up, the worse it got for me inside. I knew that I had to find a way to pull myself out of this and put fun back into my life or I would die working, but I was at a complete loss as to how to make this happen. I dared not admit to anyone that my life was less than perfect.

One day, my neighbor began to gush at how amazing my life must be. She went on to share her perception of my life as exciting, successful, filled with joy, and basically "perfect." I smiled and laughed... ah, if she only knew the internal turmoil that was occurring that very moment. One thing I can say with certainty is that I was *very good* at creating an illusion that exuded anything but what was truly going on inside me. I was beginning to implode, and I could feel the weight of everything crashing down on me. Perfect life? Hardly. The bottom line was that I was unhappy. I was losing my zest for everything, and when I looked into a mirror I was no longer sure of who I was or why I was working so hard. I did not like the person that I had become. The lack of fun and opportunities to enjoy things outside of work had become increasingly unhealthy, and I knew that this was the result of habits I had developed over the years.

Our daily activities are all centered around habits that either serve us well or do not. Habits are the result of behaviors that have been reinforced over time. For example, my habit of working out is reinforced by the increased energy I feel, the physical health I maintain, and the confidence I have when I feel good in my clothes. What then was reinforcing my workaholic approach to living? Maybe it was occupying every single minute of my day to prevent any down time that might allow things that were bothering me to creep into my consciousness. Maybe it was seeking approval from others. Or maybe it was a deep subconscious issue of feeling like I did not deserve to have fun until I had achieved certain levels of success. I would need to look inward and search for what was reinforcing my inability to jump off the proverbial hamster wheel

What could I do to put a little fun back into my life and make time for play so I would not lose my mind chasing my dreams? The ability to have fun and joy in one's life is a mindset... it's a way of thinking that you can adjust at any given moment. This seemed overwhelming to me. Thank goodness for my dogs!

BOLO makes it so easy to have fun. It's the essence of who she is. Watching her and how she interacts with the world around her showed me how much joy can come from engaging in something you absolutely love to do. During an outing to the local dog beach, I marveled at how happy she was racing along the sand, greeting other dogs, and chasing a few random seagulls. Always with a ball in her mouth, BOLO finds a way to play on her own by putting it down and digging frantically in the sand. She will create a trench into which she dives in nose first to retrieve her favorite toy. Spending time with the dogs motivated me, but I admit that making time for play continued to be a challenge every day. I would have to take baby steps to relearn what brought laughter to my heart. I knew how important spending time away from work with family and friends was to my mental and physical health. Doing this was totally up to me, and being proactive on this matter would determine whether or not I would enjoy life ahead.

I started to write a list of all the fun places I wanted to visit and things I wanted to experience. I began to say yes to invitations to baseball games, summer BBQ's, "girls night out," and even found myself addicted to a Netflix series—something mindless that would take my attention off work. I sought out comedy clubs and took time to watch the comedy channel so that I could experience what it felt like to really laugh again. By scheduling in more down time, more play time, and being present to fully enjoy these moments, I would become re-inspired, reignite my creativity, enhance my relationships, and empower myself to accomplish everything I dreamed possible.

"Have regular hours for work and play; make each day both useful and pleasant, and prove that you understand the worth of time by employing it well. Then youth will bring few regrets, and life will become a beautiful success."

~ Louisa May Alcott, Little Women

- Change your routine and habits to let fun back into your life: Give yourself permission to check out of your to-do list. During your work day, take time out to watch something funny on YouTube, go to lunch with a friend, sit in a park and watch kids play, turn up some music and jam out for a few minutes, or connect by phone with someone who always makes you laugh. Say yes to invitations from others to get out and do something fun. Make a list of new things you want to try like a cooking class, a dance class, or take a hot air balloon ride. Make a list of places to visit like an amusement park, a museum, or a comedy club. Make a list of events to experience like a baseball game, a music concert, or a Broadway show. Do something completely spontaneous.

- Schedule "stay-cations", mini-vacations, and a dream vacation: Take time to separate yourself from work and the routine of daily responsibilities. You don't have to travel far to have fun, and you don't have to fill every minute with something to do either. Just learn to relax and pick a few things that you know you will enjoy. Most people don't realize how much fun they can have at home or in a two-hour drive. Organize a neighborhood party complete with potluck dishes and games from your childhood like kickball, freeze tag, ghost in the graveyard, and kick the can. Invite some friends over for an afternoon marathon of chick flicks followed by dinner out at a favorite restaurant or bar. Take time to plan ahead for an event or getaway and then book a few long weekends throughout the year. and plan ahead for an event or getaway. Find a way to take at least one longer vacation where you can really unplug and get back to your inner child.

- Learn to be in the moment: There is nothing worse than being somewhere fun (like the beach) and missing the experiences of crashing waves, kids playing, and the feeling of the sand through your toes as you walk along the shore because your mind is at work. Conversely, it is just as debilitating to be at work and find yourself wishing you were at the beach. Give yourself permission to be present. Tell yourself you WILL be present.

- Make sure to spend time with others who are spontaneous, can laugh at themselves, really know how to enjoy any activity, want to try something new, and know how to make the distinction between work and play. They will help to increase your fun quotient.

Chapter Five

Think Big, Recognize Opportunity, and Go For It

-5-

Dogs always come from a place of abundance—especially in the case of food. They seem to know whenever it's present and assume it's theirs for the taking. In my own household, the dogs turn up their noses at miniscule crumbs on the floor. Why waste the effort focused there when bigger opportunities can be found above eye level. Over time, the prizes in my home have included salmon on the kitchen table, an entire cake prepared for a catered event, an entire plate of hors d'oeuvres—without the victim ever noticing—and Fig Newton cookies from the hands of a toddler. My dogs have been the happy beneficiaries of my harried routine. Regardless of how satiated they feel, they recognize opportunity when food is around and they sense my brain is pre-occupied. I'll confess, as a dog trainer, it pains me to admit my failure to thwart food-stealing and counter-surfing. Of the four dogs in my life, Henry is the only one who does not steal food. I believe the only reason is that he simply can't reach.

Zoe remained lean and fit up until Abby was about a year. Her controlled diet, limited access to treats, and regular exercise maintained her weight and "girlish figure." Zoe was quite unimpressed with the addition of Abby to our lives. She basically tolerated her until she discovered the baby did in fact have some utility. Zoe learned very quickly that the best place to plant herself was beneath this tiny human's high chair. From Zoe's perspective, the baby was the ideal food delivery system. Abby delighted in the response Zoe gave to every Cheerio, animal cracker, or green pea thrown on the floor. Despite Zoe's ulterior motives to snag snacks out of Abby's hands, Abby loved that the dog happily trotted by her side from room to room.

Sasha was the queen of counter surfing. She acquired this skill after walking through the kitchen and discovered grilled chicken breasts and steaks left unguarded on a plate. The countertops in this particular home were just barely above her head, and the immediate access to freshly grilled meat awaiting transfer to a dinner table was an instant jackpot. She "scarfed" it all, leaving nothing for the main dish at the small dinner party about to begin. And so began her career as the official counter-surfer and trash-can-cleaner.

Over the years, Sasha would become a master of her "trade." Everyone knew her as the sweetest, gentlest, and most loving dog you would ever meet. She was also smart and a wee bit conniving. It was not beneath her to quietly work her way through a party and stealthily snag food off of people's plates. In situations where you saw her approaching, she would work her charm as though she was coming over just to say hello and grace you with her sweetness. A new guest would not be aware of her tactics and would then lean in to pet her and tell her how sweet she was, at which point she would clean off whatever food had been on their plate. I remember being absolutely mortified as I watched her approach someone in deep conversation with another guest and immediately devour an entire piece of cake off their plate. The person never noticed, but the look on their face was priceless when they discovered it had disappeared.

BOLO is Sasha reincarnated, at least in the food-stealing department. Just like Sasha had done for years, BOLO happily greets everyone at work by first checking their trash cans to ensure nothing important was left behind. BOLO is smart. Her food-stealing often involves proper calculation and timing to get exactly what she is after—nothing is safe when she is in this mode. The first twelve months of her life in our home were very controlled. As I prepared her for her role as a future Leader Dog for the Blind, she was never unattended and had a solid response to the cue, "Leave it." Once she was "career-changed" and returned to us, all bets were off. With such a well-mannered and trained dog, no one ever thought to keep a watchful eye on her around food. I don't recall exactly when the first incident occurred, but I could write an entire coffee table book about how adept she had become at "thinking big and recognizing opportunity."

Following an evening out at dinner with friends, I brought home leftover salmon, my favorite. I took it out of the fridge the next morning so I would not forget to take it to work and placed it on the kitchen table in a spot where it would be impossible (or so I thought) for BOLO to reach and then headed off to the gym. She curled up on the rug on the floor, creating the illusion that she was just going to chill out and rest up for the day ahead. I believe the moment I started my car, she got up to look out the window, watched my car disappear, and then raced into action. She knew something delectable was awaiting her. Also in the bag to bring to work was a candle, which made the bag relatively heavy. A small portion of the bag had been placed on a pile of papers that I thought were out of reach. BOLO is very clever and managed to figure out how to slide the pile of stuff very carefully without pulling it out from under the bag and losing her only delivery option. In the process, she knocked over a full cup of coffee, which became wedged between a chair and the table. Undeterred, she continued to maneuver the pile of paper closer to the edge until she could grab the handle of the bag, take it up to my room, and begin to devour the lunch I had been looking forward to eating.

She continued to add to her "resume" on a number of occasions. There was the time she consumed an entire cake I had prepared for our holiday party, making sure to give it back to me in regurgitated form on my office floor the next morning. On another occasion, after running into the grocery store, I returned to my car to discover a dog that appeared to be foaming at the mouth and the tag of a Hershey's Kiss hanging out the corner of her "lab jowls" like a cigar. Let's be clear, there would never be any uneaten Hershey's Kisses in my car; my sugar cravings made sure of that. However, for the life of me, I could not figure out what was going on around her mouth until I discovered she had torn open a bag of flour left in the car from an earlier trip to the grocery store. The next morning, she delivered a ball of dough to my bedroom floor.

"If you're going to be thinking, you may as well think big."

~ Donald Trump

At a conference I recently attended, I was having lunch with six other people. Led by a facilitator, the conversation was about vision and preparing for opportunity. Some of the people had crystal clear visions and shared the incredibly huge goals they had set to make their vision a reality. Others were not certain of what their end game looked like and were seeking guidance to help distill it down. My attention was drawn to the people who were "thinking really big." They seemed so emotionally charged. Secretly, I thought some of these visions were quite lofty and wondered if they really believed they would reach their goals.

Quietly I thought about my vision, and suddenly it seemed small. My vision was based around my own beliefs of what was possible for me. These limiting beliefs were preventing me from thinking big and blinding me to various opportunities. How could I break through these self-imposed limitations?

"Think big and don't listen to people who tell you it can't be done. Life's too short to think small."

~ Tim Ferriss

It was time to think bigger than I ever had before, both professionally and personally. I wanted a vision that I could really get excited about, something that would inspire me every day. I had already seen first-hand how we were touching lives through our messaging and how our Dog is Good creations resonated immediately on such a personal level with dog lovers. With my "business hat" on, I looked into the future to see Dog is Good as a multimillion dollar, internationally recognized brand that brought joy to dog lovers around the world. I began to see our phenomenal headquarters equipped with the most incredible doggie daycare facility so everyone could have their dogs at work. I saw an international community of dog lovers growing and engaged with a variety of content provided by Dog is Good through services and web-based programs. I worked with Jon to set goals for Dog is Good that initially seemed out of reach but would prepare us for new and more expansive opportunities.

It was a bit more difficult for me to formulate a vision for my personal life. . Fear was an obstacle, and I struggled to move it out of the way. As I searched to find a way to shift gears in my life, I was scared of disappointing others and feared disapproval. I feared failure, falling short of others' expectations, and change. But I was at the point where the pain of where I was finally became greater than the fear that was holding me back and preventing me from exploring new adventures.

"Life is inherently risky. There is only one big risk you should avoid at all costs, and that is the risk of doing nothing."

~ Denis Waitley

I was ready to think, and so I sat down to write my big vision. I began by envisioning the house and its location on where I would make it my home. I made a list of activities I wanted to enjoy, places where I would travel, philanthropic endeavors I would pursue, new things I wanted to learn, and the material things I wanted to acquire. With my long list complete, I filled it in with great detail to create a vision much bigger than my conscious mind could have previously imagined. Once again, I set goals and became very aware of the opportunities that were presenting themselves. Every morning and every night, the vision ran through my head like a movie. For the first time in a long time, I believed anything was possible.

Now it was time to take action steps that would open doors of opportunity. I would have to train myself to think differently. I started to recognize new opportunities and became brave enough to start the pursuit that would move me closer to achieving my personal goals.

- To create a bigger vision, assess where you are right now and look five years into the future. What are you doing? Where do you live? How do you spend your time and who do you share it with? Add in all the fine details as if you are already there. Once you have the big picture in your mind, commit it to writing, and then visualize your life as it will actually become.

- Begin to work backwards to establish the your goals and identify the action steps required to get you to the end game. Be prepared to encounter obstacles and setbacks yet maintain an unwavering belief in your vision as you pursue these goals. The bigger you think, the more you attract naysayers who want to "save you from disappointment" or become judgmental as they see you making changes.

- Opportunities may not appear in the form you are expecting. As you continue to affirm your goals and visualize the future, pay attention to recurring thoughts or follow up on a hunch. The messages coming from your subconscious may be exactly the opportunity that you have failed to notice in the past.

- Be disciplined enough not to jump at every opportunity that comes your way, yet be decisive enough to take immediate action when the right ones present themselves.

"If you're offered a seat on a rocket ship, don't ask what seat! Just get on."

~Sheryl Sandberg

Chapter Six

Be Persistent and Dig Deep

-6-

be persistent.

A dog that wants something badly becomes the epitome of persistence. We were living on the Navy Base in Panama City Beach, Florida when I adopted sweet Sasha. Shortly after we moved there, I got involved with the local animal shelter and soon became the volunteer coordinator. Like many others who support rescue and strive to improve animal welfare, I started spending quite a bit of time at the facility. Before backing me up with his support, Jon reminded me that we were a "one dog" family and made me promise that it would stay that way. "Yea, sure...of course" was my casual reply.

One of my responsibilities as volunteer coordinator was to select a dog or a cat to appear on the local TV station's Pet of the Week Segment. This was a great opportunity to showcase a wonderful pet and share information about the other animals available at the shelter. Once featured on TV, it was not unusual to have several families calling the shelter to adopt the dog. In situations where no one called, I would foster the dog until a forever family arrived, which usually did not take long. I felt strongly that once I took a dog out of "prison" on adventure, there was no way I would ever surrender them back. Sasha was one of these dogs. When no one initially stepped forward to adopt her, I brought her back to the house. Weeks had gone by when my daughter commented on how long she had been in our home and wondered if we were going to keep her. At this point, we had been "fostering" her for six weeks, and I was perfectly okay with formalizing an adoption. Thinking back to my promise that we would remain a one-dog family, I told my daughter not to say a word about Sasha to her daddy. At this point, I felt she had become our dog by default. Several weeks later Jon asked, "Hey, is anyone going to adopt this dog?" to which I replied, "Yes, she has been adopted...by us! As you can see, she is the perfect dog!"

Zoe was persistent in getting attention, but Sasha's instinctive drive to hunt made her the most persistent dog of all. One of my most vivid memories occurred one weekend on our morning run. Almost every Saturday, the entire family would head out for a six-mile run around the Navy Base. At the time, our daughter was four and could still fit in the baby jogger. The dogs knew the routine and would patiently wait while we gathered up Abby's Tupperware cup filled with Cheerios, her little books, her special blanket and even a tape recorder to play Disney tunes. We would then load Abby and all of her "stuff" into the jogger and head out the door. The dogs would trot alongside of us on the vacant road that paved the entire perimeter of the base. Except for the rare appearance of the security vehicles, no cars traveled on this road, so it was quite safe to let the dogs run off leash. On the first straightaway, Zoe spent her energy racing the motorcycles traveling on the road just on the other side of the fence. Sasha paid no attention and kept moving forward with us toward the base entrance where a man-made pond was home to three resident ducks.

On this particular day, one of the ducks was walking close to the road. Yea, you know where I'm going with this. The moment my hound/pointer/spaniel mix noted the close proximity of this duck, instinctive drive took over and she bolted toward it. The poor duck immediately ran to the pond, jumped in, and started to swim away. With the duck now out of reach, I expected Sasha to rejoin us on the run; I was mistaken.

Sasha was locked onto the duck and was pacing back and forth along the water's edge. The next thing I heard was the splash of water as she jumped into the pond to continue the chase. This duck decided to have some fun with her and started swimming along. Although I could not see them, I was imagining its little feet paddling frantically in the water. This duck stayed just far enough in front of Sasha but the moment she started getting too close, the duck would just flap its wings and put an additional 2-3 feet between them. Inevitably, the duck would reach the end of the pond, prompting it to turn around, fly just above Sasha's head, and land a foot behind her. Undeterred, Sasha would just turn around and resume doggy paddling. This went on for quite a while, the duck going back and forth and Sasha maintaining persistence. Initially, we were impressed with her tenacity, but then our patience began to give way. No matter how many times I called to her, she just would not stop. I started to notice she was getting tired and wondered how long she could keep up her pursuit. It became clear she would continue the pursuit for as long as the duck kept the apparent game in play. This dog was not going to give up. She remained persistent despite her fatigue and was prepared to swim back and forth as many times as it took to get that duck. At this point, nothing was going to stop her but me. The only way I was going to get her was to take off my running shoes and swim out to grab her, which I did. She responded with a startled surprise, as though I had just shaken her out of a trance. Sasha seemed hypnotized by the entire experience. In fact, during the time I was swimming toward her in the water, she never once noticed me. Quite frankly, I was startled by the action, too. I'm not much for swimming, especially in murky water.

"You aren't going to find anybody that's going to be successful without making a sacrifice and without perseverance."

~ Lou Holtz

According to the dictionary persistence is defined as "persisting, especially in spite of opposition, obstacles, discouragement." The ability to maintain persistence can be distilled down to discipline and habits. I consider myself to be an incredibly disciplined person, almost too disciplined- if there is such a thing. Like a dog with a bone, once I set goals and put my mind to work, I become obsessive about it. Discipline combined with my persistent approach to everything I do has actually served me well throughout life. As we moved every two-three years, it would be my persistence in making the most of every new situation that resulted in unique experiences and formed friendships everywhere we lived. My persistence and disciplined approach to marketing my businesses and services helped to establish myself quickly and grow these businesses successfully in a short period of time.

Persistence begins with good habits and continues to grow through your ability to stay disciplined, but all of this boils down to the "WHY" behind your decision to go after anything. When your reasons for pursuing any goal are strong enough, you do whatever it takes to get there. I have come across a lot of people who start something only to stop as soon as life gets in the way. Obstacles are inevitable...we all encounter them, but for some, they stop the game cold and for others they are game changers. I see this every January at the gym with the influx of "New Year's Resolution" members. By March, most have already given up on their weight loss and fitness goals. In this example, losing weight and improving health was apparently just not that important to them. There are a gazillion excuses people come up with to give up on their weight loss program, stop working out, quit looking for a new job, never launch a business, finishing their education, etc.

People publicly announce their goals to ask for a promotion, get back into a pair of jeans, run a marathon, climb a mountain, start a business, go back to school, or hey, even writing a book. Initially, the drive to go after any of these things is really strong and there is belief the end result will bring success, happiness, wealth, weight loss, longevity and confidence. You are excited and find it easy to head out of the gate running towards your destination. As you do all of the right things, you gain traction towards your goal. But then a challenge arises. Someone says something to break your confidence; your friends insist you have that piece of cake to celebrate; it's raining outside so you blow off your training run; you forgo the hike with your friends to catch up on a work project over the weekend. You set yourself up for success, and then you just stop.

Why do you stop? The real reason you don't persist is simply that your *WHY* is not strong enough and you never developed disciplined habits. The pain of where you are now is not great enough to make the sacrifices necessary to see the change you want in yourself.

When Jon and I started Dog is Good, we did so with the intention of growing it to become an internationally recognized lifestyle brand for dog lovers. In building the business, growth often occurred according to the plan. Like many small business owners curve balls thrown our way created challenges, which required a course adjustment. Jon and I have always said, "It's a good thing we both never wanted to 'throw in the towel' on the same day." Why is it that I don't quit when things happen that are completely out of my control? Because I want to grow the company I started with my husband into a multimillion dollar international business. Achieving this goal will give me the opportunity to give back the bigger gift I want to share: helping others live happy and successful lives based on all that I have learned in the process of growing a start-up business inspired by Dog.

In addition to my persistence in growing our family business, I made the choice to persist everyday in learning more about myself and focus on the person I intended to be. I decided to make a change, and I knew this would require serious attention to the development of new habits. If I was going to chase my dreams, stay focused on the journey, and surround myself with the right people, then I better damn well commit to myself, to dig deep within for what I needed to do to get what I wanted. I needed to persist every single day no matter what obstacle rolled into my path.

I get up between 4:00 and 4:30 every day. I know, it sounds absurd, but I actually wake up naturally. I'm sure reading this, my husband is wondering why then do I set an alarm to ensure he is pulled out of his slumber at 4 as well? I set it just in case. Previously, my immediate action was to address work-related items on my to-do list, but now in recent months it became imperative for me to rediscover myself and seek out the core of the person I once was. Getting proactive to shift the direction of my life became so compelling that I had to establish a ritual that involved reading, visualization, and writing in a gratitude journal before starting the day. Experts say it takes 21 days to form a habit. Guess what? They are right! For the first couple weeks, this new routine was hard. The temptation to address work issues going on in my head was pretty strong, and I had to tell myself, "No, no, no, you made a decision. You wanted to change. You will keep walking past that computer, sit your butt down on that couch, and read." But then it got easier and now many months later it is a solid habit so much so that this routine never changes. Nothing is easy...NOTHING.

"Discipline is the bridge between goals and accomplishments"

~ Jim Rohn

- Before you get started with anything, you have to be crystal clear on exactly what you want.

- The burning desire to hit your target is going to be based on your WHY. This plays a direct role in the strength of your motivation. Recall a time when you were so intrinsically motivated to accomplish something that you allowed nothing to stop you. The change you will experience by reaching your goal must be compelling enough to keep you moving forward in the face of challenges.

- Create a solid action plan. The only way you can persist is to have a very clear map to follow. Establishing goals and breaking them down into manageable steps gives you objectives to meet. This becomes the "how" behind the "what" and the "why." Tell someone your goals and report to them on your progress to stay accountable. Make sure this person is positive, supportive, and encouraging. At moments when you doubt yourself, it helps to talk to someone who believes in you.

- Quit worrying what other people will think or say. Do whatever you can to remove negative thoughts and spend less time with negative people. Identify the fears that hold you back, forcing you to put on the brakes the moment things get difficult.

Chapter Seven

If It's Worth Doing, It's Worth Overdoing

-7-

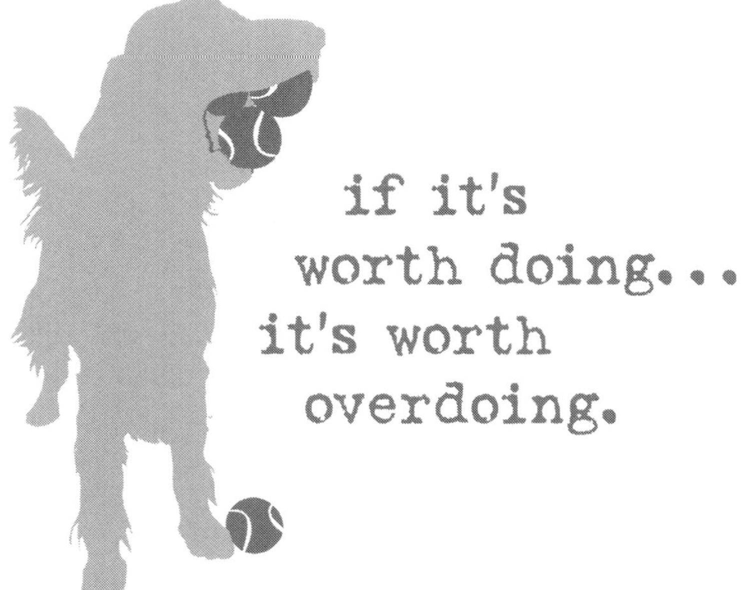

if it's
worth doing...
it's worth
overdoing.

For those of you who are currently (or have been at some point) a parent of a teenager, you may relate to the experience I had one morning. Let me preface this story by saying that I am fortunate to have an easygoing, respectful, and genuinely good-natured teen. However, I have to wonder sometimes why she chooses which activities/tasks will receive 100% of her effort.

On this particular day, I came downstairs to discover the previous night's dinner plates, etc. on the counter near the dishwasher. Her chore was to empty the dishwasher. After doing so, she neglected to take the dirty dishes and put them in the now-empty dishwasher. Other than using the excuse that she is a "teenager," I don't know why she avoided the obvious next step. Yet, I do know, if it had been something she enjoyed, she would have gone above and beyond the "call of duty." It begged the question, why do *anything* at a level less than 100%?

Dogs always seem to go all out (and then some) with everything they do. They don't just trot toward a thrown ball—they race with intention and excitement. They don't just lightly paw at the earth to get something below—they dig enthusiastically. They don't just welcome you home with a quick fly-by sniff of your clothing and a lame tail wag—they are exuberant, offering up full body wags, kisses, and power tail wags. They even put forth maximum effort to disguise themselves in "war paint." Let me explain...

On a recent walk, in a safe area where the dogs run off-leash, BOLO managed to discover wild animal poop. Deep in conversation, Jon and I did not notice, until she ran past us. As we continued walking and talking, the stench took us over. BOLO, a once beautiful yellow lab, had been transformed into a light chocolate-colored lab. To her delight, she had discovered a huge pile of animal feces. She chose not to engage in the "standard rolling of shoulder/neck area" in the poop but instead chose to go "all out" and roll her **ENTIRE** body in this disgusting animal mess. Dogs roll in feces to disguise their scent and "blend in" during the "hunt." Now completely camouflaged, even BOLO recognized that she was repulsive and tried desperately to remove the vile excrement by rolling around in ground coverage. Her efforts backfired, and she only managed to grind the stuff more deeply into her fur. Realizing that she was not getting rid of the stench, she jumped up, looked alert and happy, and proceeded to search for the next rabbit or ground squirrel to chase. This little setback was not going to deter her fun, cause her to change plans, or frustrate her. Instead, she shook off what she could and headed off in the direction of a ground squirrel racing across the pavement to get to its hole in the ground. I'll spare you the awful details of driving home with her in the car, but suffice it to say, it took SEVERAL showers to get the mess and stench off of her.

My point is that BOLO and all the other dogs I have ever worked with not only go after what they want, but they go at it with 100% effort. If my daughter approached the kitchen chore in the same vein as BOLO approached rolling in animal poop, not only would the dishes have been in the dishwasher, but the entire kitchen would have likely been immaculate. If it's worth doing, it's worth overdoing.

"No one ever attains very eminent success by simply doing what is required of him; it is the amount and excellence of

what is over and above the required, that determines the greatness of ultimate distinction."

~ Charles Francis Adams

I am blessed with many wonderful friends. One such friend comes to mind when I think about the sentiment, "If it's worth doing...it's worth overdoing". This woman has many talents and a special gift for touching everyone around her. I know my life has been affected with such lasting impact because of the added thought and care that goes into everything she does. As I think about the types of experiences I want to create as an employer, a wholesaler, a retailer, a friend, a parent, and a spouse, I often think about the magic she infuses into every project, party, craft, or gift she creates.

Following a cutback at the local hospital where she worked, she chose to take time off from full time employment to enjoy and be fully available for her daughter who was graduating from high school in a short 18 months. I was fortunate that she chose to spend part of her days here at Dog is Good where she had fun, enjoyed a flexible schedule, and became an integral part of our company's growth. She was happy to be here and, together with another one of my friends, was responsible for turning our warehouse into a comedic fun zone filled with a lot of laughter. While I was running around trying to get through the gazillion things on my to-do lists, I was keenly aware of her wonderful ability to turn the ordinary into the extraordinary.

From the moment I met her nine years ago until now, she has consistently wowed me, and everyone else, with her detailed approach to even the simplest of things.

One of my earliest memories in our friendship was getting the chance to celebrate the 4th of July with her family and four others. A skilled photographer, she spent the evening clicking away on her camera, capturing every moment throughout the evening. Two days later, she showed up at my home with a beautifully wrapped gift. She said it was just a little something she threw together to thank me for including her family in a fabulous 4th of July celebration. I opened the package to discover a beautiful shadow box picture frame with a photo of Jon, Abby, and me, and cute decorations that she had taken the time to buy and attach inside the frame. This provided a 3D element to enhance the picture and commemorate the event.

This was special—she did not just give me photos from the evening, she sat down and created something that to this very day remains in my kitchen. That picture frame was just the beginning. In the years since, I observed how "overdoing" something touched many hearts and certainly made a huge difference in the experiences people had.

We both laugh now at a situation where one of my own dogs almost thwarted her efforts in pulling off an activity for the Girl Scout Daddy-Daughter dance that she was putting together. She needed a large facility for this event, and I was able to get her access to the recreational building on the Navy Base where we lived. To help make things easier for her setup day, I offered to store items in my garage on base so that she would not have to drive back and forth numerous times to her home. In addition to tons of arts and crafts items, she also had several Marie Callender's pies for the event, which she planned on putting in my extra refrigerator. Yes, once again, you may know where I am going with this story. As we talked (away from her open car), Sasha had managed to jump into the back hatch to devour the pies. We realized what was happening and frantically ran over screaming to get her out of the car. Fortunately, many pies were saved, and her event went off famously. As I would learn, anything this woman touched was transformed into something quite memorable.

Having her on board at Dog is Good meant events hosted at work turned into projects of impeccable presentation. Together with another fabulous and talented woman at work, Dog is Good never hosted a typical warehouse sale or party. Much care and thought would be placed on every detail, and nothing was ever done in any ordinary manner.

Take the Dog is Good holiday party that was held in my home. The only holiday decoration I owned was a menorah. Despite pleas from my daughter, I never gave into requests for a "Hanukkah Bush" or blue lights to put up outside. When she learned that the party was at my home, her eyes widened with excitement. She knew I would never come close to being confused for Martha

Stuart, so she jumped at the chance to transform my home. She was a busy elf that day, showing up with a carload of decorations and sleeves rolled up. I came home later to discover the most gorgeously decorated and festive home that was warm and inviting. She truly made the event a memorable extravaganza complete with lots of ooohs and aaaahs from everyone.

The most touching event of all was her generosity in joining forces with my other friends at work to host a very personal birthday party for me. I have never been more moved by the attention to detail that she took on every element of the celebration. Tables were embellished with whimsical purple table clothes, my favorite color. Centerpieces were constructed from photos of me with BOLO—who was soon returning to Leader Dogs for the Blind to continue her guide dog program. The food table had other decor significant to my personality. The experience brought tears to my eyes, and I felt overwhelmed by how all the added touches made me feel special and important. The experience was forever burned into my memory as a reminder of how exceeding expectations can make a memorable impact.

I find the statement, "How you do anything is often how you do everything" very impactful. When we make a decision to do something, we can chose to make the experience good, or we can make it extraordinary! Taking the time to provide that extra touch is what differentiates between average and amazing. Going *beyond* excellent makes your personal involvement in something more valuable, and the experience it creates for others is simply unforgettable. Staying true to my reputation as an overachiever, I want to be the best—or at least offer more than my best—as a spouse, mom, friend, and business owner.

I am nowhere near as creative as my friend, but I am a firm believer in raising the bar on how you interact with other, approach personal goals, and your business or job performance is perceived. I always strive to exceed people's expectations For the past several months, all I was overdoing was overscheduling my life and increasing my workload. This made it impossible for me to infuse creativity in the projects I was working on. I was overdoing it all right, to the point of such extreme burnout that nothing I touched or did was memorable. My challenge would be to figure out a way to stop the insanity. I am fully cognizant of the fact that I need to be more present, improve my organizational skills, slow down, stop multitasking, and think through what it takes to make experiences special. I am learning to differentiate between overdoing it in terms of scheduling more than is humanly possible to accomplish and overdoing it on a task, project, etc...to create a lasting positive impact.

Life is all about the experience. Why shouldn't each and every experience we create for ourselves or others be anything less than memorable?

"Excellence is doing ordinary things extraordinarily well."

~ John W. Gardner

- Put forth better than average effort into anything you do. It does not matter if you are cleaning your kitchen, working on a project from work, or hosting an event—you are already spending the time and energy anyway.

- To make yourself or an experience more memorable, be thoughtful in your approach, taking things from satisfactory to extraordinary.

- Write a personal note or tell someone in person how their efforts to go above and beyond your expectations have made a lasting impression on you and others.

Chapter Eight

Make Things Happen

-8-

Dogs have an uncanny way of getting what they want. They do what works for them and find that it's quite easy to "train" the families they live with. Dogs are masters at getting you to respond to their relentless quest for attention, treats, or playtime. Whether it's dropping a ball at your feet, picking up their leash to go for a walk, or scratching at a door to be let out, dogs know exactly what to do to get what they want. Some would call this manipulation...I agree. Zoe was a master manipulator.

Eight years into the adventure of being a Navy wife, we got word that we were going to be moving overseas. Jon was taking command of a ship at the Navy base in Sasebo, Japan. I was excited about the idea of living in a foreign country. Once there, I made many new friends, immersed myself in the culture, and enjoyed daily adventures on the beautiful island, which seemed like paradise to me. Although it was incredibly fun, I felt something was missing. Having a baby was not in my immediate future but with Jon's deployments at sea and his need to attend to a demanding job, I longed for something to care for. One morning, there it was: the ad in the local base paper advertising FREE puppies to a good home. There were not many dogs in the city of Sasebo, and it was a grueling process to get dogs from the USA to Japan. However, two Navy families living next to each other in base housing had managed to bring their beloved pets with them on this overseas tour. They soon found themselves responsible for a litter of puppies, the result of the budding romance between one family's black lab and the other family's Dalmatian. I have strong feelings about spaying and neutering to prevent unwanted litters, but this is not the book for a lecture on responsible dog ownership.

At the time, I knew nothing about dogs. I had not grown up around dogs, nor did I ever desire one until that moment. I called Jon at work to tell him about these puppies. His immediate response was, "No way, we are not getting a dog." I pleaded and told him I just wanted to look at sweet puppies and promised I would not beg like a 10-year-old once we were there. As most husbands do, he broke down; Jon had grown up with a dog, so I figured he felt a little nostalgic and desired a little puppy breath too. Once we hung up the phone, I immediately called my friend to let her know that we were going to be getting a puppy. She was a little surprised to hear the news, as she knew Jon and his practicality. She asked if he said yes to my plea and laughed at my response. Of course he did not say yes to the puppy, but he *did* say that we could go look. I knew it would be impossible to "just look" at a litter of adorable puppies and not go home with one. I was convinced that I would soon become the doting mom to a new puppy. With no knowledge of dogs, dog behavior, puppy raising, etc, I did exactly what I warn people not to do and adopted a puppy because it was cute and I wanted something to nurture.

Into our home came the most adorable white puppy with perfectly symmetrical black ears. Her spots would appear later (something I did not know about Dalmatians). She was simply irresistible and had me under her spell the moment she arrived.

One of the first rules Jon insisted upon was that the dog would never be allowed in the bed. I agreed because I was just thrilled to have a puppy. This would be the first of many rules to be broken. Zoe became an expert at making things happen and was one of the best trainers I've known. Early on, I taught her to ring a bell that hung by the door whenever she wanted to go out. I was so proud of myself for teaching her this skill that I promptly got up and raced to the door every time she rang the bell. Housetraining seemed under control, and then she started to abuse the system, ringing the bell constantly just so she could go outside. After a few weeks, I suddenly realized that she had me at her beck and call.

Because I knew nothing about dog training, Zoe continued to rule her environment both in and out of the home. I had no idea that if you call a dog to come to you at the dog park or when it is outside playing that it will quickly learn that coming to you means all the fun has to end. On numerous occasions, the moment it was time to leave, she would take off. She wanted to continue to chase her balls or the Canadian geese that often frequented an open field where we played. Jon and I would be at our wit's end driving up and down the park's adjacent road with the door to our minivan open trying to get this dog into the van. She was fully entertained and having the time of her life playing with us. It was only when she was truly tired and ready to go that she would willingly trot over and jump in the van as though the past 20 minutes were no big deal.

Zoe's antics did not stop at the dog park. With the addition of a beautiful new baby in our home, Zoe took advantage of every opportunity to make sure all attention remained on her. Likely no surprise to seasoned dog lovers and trainers, Zoe would immediately engage in "attention seeking behavior" anytime I was interacting with the baby. Whenever I sat down to feed Abby, she would bring me her ball and bark at me until I threw it to the other side of the great room in our home. She would race to get it and always dropped it a few feet away, forcing me to get up out of the chair to walk over and get it. On one occasion, when I was tired of getting up and down with a nursing baby in my arms, she picked up that ball, put it in front of a piece of furniture, purposefully pushed it underneath, and then proceeded to bark incessantly as she attempted to gain access to it. Without realizing how well she trained me, the only way I could stop the annoying barking was to get up, put the baby down, get on my hands and knees, and reach under the furniture to get her ball. There was no question this dog knew exactly what she was doing. She continued to make things happen for herself until the day I decided to go to school to become a professional dog trainer.

Like dogs, kids also seem to know how to make things happen for themselves. My daughter demonstrated this skill time and time again. Her ability to "make things happen" resulted in the addition of Henry, the Japanese Chin; a hamster; and a guinea pig. Abby spent the first four years of her life with just Zoe. Sasha joined our family shortly after her 4th birthday. Zoe and Sasha were technically my dogs, and she longed to have a puppy of her own. She asked the one parent she knew would say yes to a new puppy-me. She would have to find a way to get her father on board and, because he was not as enthusiastic, she realized she had her work cut out for her.

Trying to narrow down the various dogs that would be easy to assimilate into the family, she began her research to identify temperaments, traits, and grooming and exercise requirements. I am not kidding when I tell you this 8-year-old spent countless hours reading books and learning about every single dog breed to make the right selection. Despite numerous conversations on what she was learning, Jon remained steadfast in his feelings on adding a third dog. During this time, he had also received orders to take over as the commanding officer of the Naval Weapons Station in Seal Beach, CA. Unbeknownst to Abby, a move would occur within the year.

We chose not to tell her right away as the move was a little too far into the future, and there was no reason to worry her. Up until that point, moving Abby was easy—she was too young to have formed strong connections to any one person or location; however this time was different. She was involved in dance and synchronized swimming and had forged a number of wonderful friendships. Taking her away from this was going to be difficult.

One afternoon, after spending the entire day working on a project, she bounded down the stairs full of excitement. In her hands was her "masterpiece," a book she had written. Prominently displayed on the front cover was the title,

"The Day I Got My Own Puppy." She had drawn an adorable picture of herself playing with a puppy, and beneath it were the words: Written and Illustrated by Abby Kurtz. I was very impressed with her personal account of her quest to get her own dog. It was quite convincing—but then again, I was already sold on the idea of another dog. It was up to her to persuade her dad, and I had a funny feeling that this book would seal the deal. When Jon came home from work, I told him that Abby had written a special story about getting a puppy. He smiled at the cute book cover but was still standing firm that we would not get another dog. I told him I understood, but after he read the very detailed story, it was going to be his responsibility not only to tell her "no," but that he also planned on moving her away from her friends and the activities she loved to a place where she knew no one and would have to start over in a new school. Two months later, we welcomed Henry into the family and the rest is history.

"You can't just sit there and wait for people to give you that golden dream. You've got to get out there and make it happen for yourself."

~ Diana Ross

As a military spouse, mastering the concept of "making things happen" would be critical if I was going to enjoy each new move. In every situation, as soon as we were unpacked and settled into our new home, I looked for ways to get involved in the community, make new friends, and launch marketing initiatives so that I could build my businesses quickly. One benefit about being part of a military family is that all the other families are going through the same thing, so I found it easy to forge strong bonds with other women quickly.

It required a little more effort to jumpstart my business initiatives. When I was doing sales, I immediately looked for business prospects to put into my sales pipeline and started "smiling and dialing:" a nice way to describe cold calling. Strangers became customers, and quite a few of them became friends that I still stay in touch with today. Once I moved on from direct sales and got certified as a professional dog trainer, I would quickly find locations to hold classes and then market myself through veterinary practices, groomers, pet stores, and local parks and recreation programs. In order for me to ignite the fire under my business endeavors, I had to push any fear aside and get into action quickly.

Through all the experience I gained while "starting over" every two years, I had a strong belief in myself as a start-up entrepreneur. When the time came to launch Dog is Good, I felt equipped to do what was necessary to get it off the ground. To "make things happen," I embroidered hats, silk-screened some T-shirts, and took my inventory to sell at local dog-related events. I went every weekend to just about every dog walk, pet expo, or local fair to share my wares with the dog lovers around me. I made cold calls every day to people all over the country asking them to look at my new company and to bring products into their stores. Through the encouragement of other manufacturers, we decided to take the plunge and invest in creating a presence for Dog is Good at an industry tradeshow. Over time, the business grew, doubling in sales year over year. I spent late nights with Jon packing boxes and shipping out orders until we could hire people to take over those tasks. I continued calling potential retailers and talked to as many people as I could, building relationships that would help me learn what I needed to know to keep the upward trajectory of growth. While running a startup company is not easy, I did whatever it took to make things happen.

"It had long since come to my attention that people of accomplishment rarely sat back and let things happen to them. They went out and happened to things."

~ Leonardo Da Vinci

As I started to write a new chapter in my life, the first thing I did to start to make things happen was attend a business and personal growth conference. I had already begun to identify things I was passionate about and the conference offered a new perspective. With a greater commitment to existing business goals and a new focus on personal goals, I felt better armed with resources to help me. Taking the plunge to write this book, something I had never considered before and which frightened me, put me on the right track. I ordered a stack of books from the best business and personal development leaders and began reading and taking copious notes to follow through with my action plan. Achieving my new goals would not happen if I did not take action—an often-missing ingredient in the recipe for success. It was not enough to wish for something new. I had to make it happen for myself.

"Everything comes to those who hustle while they wait"

~ Thomas Edison

- Take responsibility to shape your destiny by boldly taking action to go after what you want.

- Stop being fearful and start taking risks. You would be amazed at the new doors that are opened just because you reached for the doorknob.

- If the goal is to get off the hamster wheel and really make some changes, look at what you are doing outside of work and sleep. Are you wasting hours in front of the TV or surfing the Internet looking at anything but the information that will put you on the right track? Do you see the weekend as your time to escape and hit the bars or head to parties with friends?

- Understand that if nothing changes, you must accept mediocrity and stop complaining. Doing everything but the actions that lead you toward your goal will lead only to regret.

- Follow through on the promises you make to yourself. Quit coming up with excuses! If you say you are going to get up 30 minutes earlier to focus on a new project or do something for yourself, then follow Nike's mantra and "just do it." If you say you are not going to work on the weekend, plan an outing to ensure you don't fall into the trap of jumping on the computer. When you begin to be true to the promises you make for yourself, it becomes much easier to make things happen in every aspect of your life.

Chapter Nine

Always Leave Your Mark

-9-

Without warning, dogs can provide you with the greatest comical moments, forever leaving their mark in your memory.

Once again we were preparing for another move: this time from the state of Washington to sunny southern

California. We decided to lighten the load by listing a good portion of our furniture on Craig's List. On the list to go was a beautiful living room set consisting of a white sofa and love seat and matching coffee and end tables. This living room set would soon be settling in the home of its third family as we had happily taken it off the hands of an army family prior to our move from Pennsylvania. We received a call from an interested family that they definitely wanted to purchase the entire set and would be over in a few hours to pick it up.

I had left home with my daughter and her synchronized swimming team on a road trip for a big competition. Jon was left behind to do some final clean up on the sofas. He spent more than two hours steam cleaning and painstakingly removing the little dog hairs that were stuck in the loosely woven flower patterns on the fabric. By the time he was finished, the set looked pristine. As he admired the fruits of his labor, brief thought was given to whether or not we should sell them but was quickly pushed aside as moves were always easier when we got rid of as much stuff as possible. With sofa and loveseat ready for sale, he moved on to the next preparations for the move.

Dogs seem to know when something is up. They pick up on the stressors we unconsciously put out into the universe, and Zoe was fully tuned into the fact that something was going on. This would be her 5th move, and she had become conditioned to learn that the vast purge of just about everything in our home meant we were leaving for new adventures. Following the completion of his other chores, Jon returned to the living room to discover Zoe sitting on the couch. This was odd. At the time, we did not have a formal rule about dogs on the furniture, but Zoe was almost never on the furniture. There would be the occasional moment one would find her curled up in a chair or sleeping on the forbidden sofa at my in-laws, but she rarely attempted to perch herself on top of this sofa. Regardless, she sat there with a blank stare, just looking at Jon. Concerned that he had to start picking hairs out of the fabric while the buyers were already on their way, he called to her to get off the couch. When he moved closer to physically shoo her away, she proceeded to scoot her behind across the newly steam-cleaned white sofa, making certain to leave her mark. Now visible to anyone looking was the brown "skid mark" she left behind.

Horrified and realizing the purchasers of the couch were going to arrive any minute, Jon scrambled to reassemble the steam-cleaning machine and find the stain remover. He worked on the freshly stained cushion, removing the evidence just in time for inspection. As a precaution, he turned the stained cushion over and could hardly keep a straight face as the family gushed at how beautiful and brand new this entire living room set appeared to be. After the goods were packed into the U-Haul and headed off to their new home, Jon called to share the story. To this day, we can't tell the "Zoe skid mark" story without busting into laughter.

Most dogs mark differently than described in the story above and do so for a number of reasons. The most common reason is as a way to mark their territory or to show dominance. Although this behavior is associated mostly with male dogs, female dogs mark territories as well. On walks, Henry stops at every vertical post, bush, rock, and tree to lift his leg and let all the other dogs in the community know that he was there. Fortunately, he is well trained and often off-leash during our walks. Without this luxury, a normal 30-minute walk could take over an hour.

Humans don't mark to stake claim to territory, thank goodness, but we do have the opportunity to leave our mark on the world around us. We are able to create lasting impressions on the people we meet, engage in random acts of kindness, provide continued support to our family and friends, and encourage others around us. How we choose to interact in any of these areas can determine the quality of our own existence and the legacy we leave behind. Everyone wants to be memorable, myself included. We may not make historic strides like Mother Teresa, Gandhi, Martin Luther King, and one of my favorites, Oprah, but we do have the opportunity to leave indelible marks behind on others.

"The purpose of life is not to be happy. It is to be useful, to be honorable, to be compassionate, to have it make some difference that you have lived and lived well."

~Ralph Waldo Emerson

When you define your personal values, identify the contributions you want to make in the world, and determine how you want your life to touch others, you are better equipped to make a lasting impact. Many of us want to feel like we make a difference and that our efforts somehow make our communities and world a better place. Participating in something greater than oneself either by giving time through volunteer work, creating awareness for a cause through social media, or donating money in support of something you believe in, are additional ways to leave a positive mark.

Think about the encounters you have during a week: the checkout people at the grocery store, the waitress at a restaurant, the gas attendant at the service station, the other parents involved in your child's activities, your child's teachers, your co-workers, your spouse, your children, and your friends. My first question is, "Are you truly present with the people in any of the suggested situations?" My second question is, "Who are you in those situations? How do you make each and everyone feel?"

Throughout the day our behaviors and words will either affect someone positively or negatively. How do you want people to feel the moment they walk away from you? How do you touch people in your daily interactions? Most of us do not intend to make others feel like crap, but sometimes our thoughtless, reactive behaviors do just that. Imagine what it must feel like to be on the receiving end of angry, impatient words or to be treated as though you did not even exist. The use of disparaging words, effusion of anger, overt disgust or impatience with others, and general disregard for another human being leaves them feeling poorly. A simple compliment, a sincere thank you, expressions of appreciation for a job well done, or basic acknowledgement of another person goes a very long way in making someone's day.

As we run around like crazy people throughout the day, showing patience, kindness, and empathy can easily leave a lasting, positive imprint on others who are also caught up in their own stressors of daily life. Your departure from any encounter with people should never leave behind carnage. We should strive always to act with integrity, show decency and respect for human beings, and help others without regard for getting something in return. In other words, live by the golden rule, "Do unto others as you would have done unto yourself."

I don't have a formal education or training in business development or leadership. My entrepreneurial spirit has put me in a position of leadership. Through my business, I have created lasting value for customers. As a result, Dog is Good is known for its exceptional customer care. I am proud of the corporate giving program we have developed at Dog is Good. I am thankful that we have been able to give generously to a variety of organizations and promote the positive effects that come as a result of the dog-human bond. It was from this mindset that I chose to be overtly involved in The BOLO Project, a program created to raise awareness for the role of service dogs and raise funds for Leader Dogs for the Blind. As I mentioned in the foreword, throwing myself wholeheartedly into this project would forever change my life. I am thankful that we have been able to benefit animal welfare organizations and promote the positive effects that come as a result of the dog-human bond.

Knowing that it is my responsibility to lead by example and promote excellence in those that work with me, both in and out of my business, I studied great leaders and sought out mentors. The positive marks left by people of influence are dependent on their personal character, integrity, humility, vision, attitude, and level of respect toward others. I wanted to learn from these individuals.

We spend a majority of our life at work, which guarantees opportunities to leave some kind of mark on our co-workers, industry associates, and customers. It's either going to be a mark of excellence or stain like a skid mark. It is up to each of us to decide.

I am a firm believer in the idea that we learn great lessons each day from our dogs but also from people in our lives. We are all given the opportunity to engage in random acts of kindness throughout each day. Some of us are very proactive, but most seem too busy to notice when these opportunities arise. I was recently so moved by a story told to me by a dear friend about her daughter. It truly defined what it means to always leave your mark.

First, a brief back-story.

We moved down to California when my daughter Abby was going into 4th grade. She was not too happy to leave her friends behind and start a new school where she didn't know anyone. As you can imagine, for a nine-year-old this isn't the easiest experience, so I decided to join her for lunch on her second day of classes. We were invited to sit down at a table with two very stereotypical California girls. As they sat across from us with their sun-kissed faces and sun-bleached blonde hair, one of the little girls welcomed us. Her name was Madison McCulloch. She asked us a lot of questions about where we came from and excitedly told us all about Seal Beach. That day, Abby and Madi became instant friends.

Fast forward eight years later: That freckle-faced little girl has grown up into a beautiful young woman who not only holds a leadership position at her high school, but also works a part time job and volunteers regularly for a number of worthy causes. Obviously, for any seventeen year-old, these are all wonderful accomplishments. What makes Madi stand out is how she leaves her mark on a daily basis, epitomizing the true spirit of humanity.

Madi works at a local coffee shop, Bogarts. She is quite personable and is a valued employee. Upon visiting the coffee shop, her mother witnessed a beautiful selfless act of kindness toward another human being. Like many communities around the country, there are individuals in Seal Beach who do not have a roof over their head, a regular place to sleep, to bathe, or to eat. One such gentleman walked into Bogarts and was greeted politely and enthusiastically by Madi. His appearance might have made others feel uncomfortable, but Madi spoke to him respectfully and energetically asked him how he was feeling that day while inquiring if he would like a cup of coffee. He graciously answered that he was doing well but needed to use the restroom.

Without hesitation, Madi pointed him in the right direction and told him that she would have a cup of coffee and a donut ready for him when he returned. She promptly poured him a cup of coffee and set a donut on the counter. When he appeared again, he took the coffee and donut and politely thanked her before leaving. Madi wished him well and told him to have a wonderful day. My friend watched her daughter in awe as all this took place and then asked how she could just give him coffee and a donut. Madi smiled at her mother and told her without a second thought that she did it all the time and that she paid for it using her own money. The tears welled up in my friend's eyes—and mine—when she told me the story.

- We all have the opportunity to do things daily that positively impact the world around us. These "things" can be as simple as a smile, lending a helping hand directly, or communicating with another human being with the respect they so deserve.

- Lead by example: This applies to how you parent as well as how you lead a team at work. We are always modeling behavior. How would you like your children or employees to behave when faced with the opportunity to help others or do something to impact positively the world around them?

- Make yourself available to touch people's lives: Rather than go about our days caught up with ourselves, our computer, the television, or our smart phones, take time to volunteer, be a voice for a child or animal without one, support an existing cause, or start one of your own. Challenge yourself to find ways to leave your mark. With this conscious effort, your home, work environment, community, and world will be a much brighter, happier, and better place because you have been there.

Chapter Ten

Celebrate the Little Things

-10-

celebrate the
little things.

For a year, I lived on the military base at the United States Army War College in Carlisle, PA. During my time there, my morning routine was very consistent. An early run and visit to the gym were followed up with breakfast and lunch preparations to get Jon fed and out the door for a full day of classes. Abby would also be fed and then delivered safely to her first grade class. After all human family members were squared away and in their perspective places, I would then take my two dogs to the dog park on the base.

This designated area for dogs was huge. It was a favorite place for me to visit with the pups. It was also home to what seemed to be the entire groundhog population of PA.

In the fall, the trees showcased their brightly colored leaves, vibrant reds, yellows, and oranges. In the spring, flowers bloomed throughout the entire open field. In the center of all this open space was a random area where chest-high grass and wild flowers densely grew. The area was about the size of a basketball court and seemed a little out of place.

On our walks every morning, Zoe and Sasha would eagerly pull me in the direction of the park. Every excursion became a training walk on impulse control and loose leash walking. It was good practice for me as a trainer. Once at the park, I would put them in their sit-stay before taking off their leashes. Both would quiver with excitement in anticipation of the pending freedom to race through the park to chase the groundhogs.

The moment the dogs took off, those groundhogs would race to the nearest hole and disappear instantly. Each dog would stay actively engaged in the hunt until there was nothing left to chase, at which point their different personalities and behavioral traits surfaced.

Zoe turned her attention toward me, barking wildly for me to toss the ball I had brought along. She would then engage in her special way of playing fetch: getting me to walk all over the park to pick up the ball that she would chase but never bring back.

Sasha, on the hand, would continue to race from hole to hole, searching for the groundhogs. There were times when my attention would be drawn to the tall reed-like grass in the center. Although I could not see her, the rapid movement of the tall grass told me she was scrambling through there, chasing rabbits or looking for those evasive groundhogs. Every so often, her head would pop through the perimeter, tongue halfway out of her mouth, and a doggie smile that seemed to express her desire to tell me, "Don't worry, Mom. I'm going to get something...just you wait."

Then it happened. One sunny morning while standing in the park, a groundhog came out of its hole, right next to Sasha. She pounced instantly and, without warning, had this poor animal in her mouth. I was HORRIFIED, but as I started screaming, I observed something interesting. Zoe started jumping up in the air, doing half twists before landing and jumping up again. While Sasha was busy engaging in her instinctive shake-and-kill, a truly horrible thing for me to witness, Zoe was ecstatic, jumping and barking as if to say "OMG! You got it! You finally got it! Hurray for you!"

Torn between the panicked, sick feeling I felt and the desire to observe animal behavior, I continued to watch as Sasha began to prance like a horse with this now-deceased animal in her mouth. Zoe trotted next to her, tail wagging, seemingly beaming with pride as she looked my way.

They were celebrating. They were celebrating the kill, an accomplishment that took months and months. I was stunned and suddenly realized I was still screaming as I raced after these two dogs. Unable to get the groundhog out of Sasha's mouth (OK, in truth, I did not try to get the huge thing out of her mouth...I just kept screaming), my screaming caught the attention of the security personnel who I convinced to get the dead animal from the grips of Sasha's jaws. Despite losing the prized possession to a stoic army guard, both dogs showed no sign of disappointment. In fact, they were charged and still excited as we made our way back home.

As I remember this story, it made me realize the importance of celebrating and recognizing accomplishments big and small. This brought up some questions: What was I doing to recognize and celebrate the people at work and the good things they were doing to help me grow my business? What was I doing to acknowledge and celebrate the successes and joyous occasions that were occurring for my friends and family? Lastly, what was I doing to take time to celebrate my own accomplishments?

I find it easy to celebrate people at Dog is Good. Both Jon and I mention to each other almost daily how fortunate we are to work with people who take great ownership and pride in the work they do to help us grow the business. Our DIG family has become such an integral part of our continued growth and success. We take immense pleasure in recognizing team members publicly for the positive impact their daily actions have on the business. Regular get-togethers for lunch and after-work parties provide opportunity to reward and celebrate significant accomplishments. More importantly, it gives us the opportunity to celebrate them as individuals and share their joy as they experience milestone events and accomplishments outside of work.

Celebrating others is much easier for me than celebrating myself. There is no question that I never slow down my manic pace to recognize my achievements. Over time, the lack of reward began to have a debilitating effect on my enthusiasm. Acknowledging key milestones and achievements in my business and in my personal life would inject the necessary "juice" to keep me motivated, enthusiastic, and inspired to continue moving forward.

I use positive reinforcement all the time when in dog training. Rewarding desired behaviors with something the dog enjoys increases the frequency and intensity of those behaviors. Conversely, when no recognition or reinforcement is provided, a behavior will decrease in intensity, frequency, and ultimately disappear over time. People are no different. The act of celebration is reinforcement. It reinforces confidence in your ability, strengthens belief in yourself, and enhances enthusiasm to try new things or tackle your next big goal. With every achievement comes opportunity for reward. If you keep moving forward time and time again without reward or celebration along the way, you risk losing the driving force behind your passion.

Jack Canfield, author of *Chicken Soup for the Soul* and *The Success Principles,* suggests taking inventory of one's successes throughout life. So, to stop the pending crash and burn, I sat down to mull over all the amazing things I have achieved over the past 50 years.

I liked this exercise because I discovered that I had a lot of things to write down. When I stepped away from the list and came back to it a few hours later, I was pretty impressed with myself. I had forgotten so many of the major breakthroughs and achievements over the course of my life. Reviewing them reminded me of my strengths and brought a renewed confidence in knowing that I really could do anything I put my mind to. In moments when I feel uncertain or I am facing greater challenges, I can look at my list of life accomplishments from simple things like holding the school record in my elementary school for the most sit-ups, or passing up Oprah in the final mile of the Marine Corps Marathon, to awards for Dog is Good, and raising a bright, talented, and well-adjusted teenager. I was also able to take stock of challenges experienced along the way and review the strategies employed to overcome them.

Once I was truly cognizant of my own accomplishments, it was easier for me to acknowledge the importance of celebrating myself and life around me. Celebration is a form of gratitude, and with gratitude in life there is more to celebrate. When you commit to searching for all things good in your life, such as the ability to wake up, get out of bed, walk with legs and feet, see with your eyes, find food in your refrigerator, have clothing in your closet to wear, stay warm with a roof over your head, have a car to drive to a business you own, and have strong relationships with people who love you, it provides you with a better lens from which to view the world.

"Promise yourself today to be just as enthusiastic about the success of others as you are about your own."

~ Christian D. Larson

There is no way to move forward in a positive way when you waste precious energy focusing on what you feel you lack or on envying others. Real power lies in the ability to celebrate success, find gratitude in your own life, and fully embrace the successes and joys occurring in the lives of others.

Social media keeps us connected to family and friends in ways that can leave one feeling as though their life is anything but exciting. After spending a long week working like a maniac, I'll admit I sometimes find myself a bit envious as I scope out photos of friends on vacation or read about major achievements of business colleagues. I am usually so excited for my friends and colleagues, but I found it more difficult in the past couple years to feel a pure intrinsic joy in celebrating what they were experiencing. Shedding the envy opens one up to embrace the accomplishments and experiences of others. When was the last time you internalized the success of others? It is actually empowering and uplifting.

There are so many ways to celebrate yourself and others.

- Start a success and gratitude journal. Take time every evening to reflect on the day's activities. In addition to recording all the things you are grateful for, highlight the big and small successes that may have occurred during the day.

- Do something that is just for you and treat yourself to something that makes you feel great: get a massage, get a mani-pedi, get your hair blown out, or plan a long weekend getaway.

- Invite friends to join you out for happy hour or dinner. Toast yourself and your recent accomplishments and then encourage everyone else to do the same.

- Celebrate other's successes and achievements at work. This can be done by publicly recognizing them at staff meetings, giving a gift card, , g rewarding with a day off with pay or flex hours, decorating their workspace, or writing them a personal congratulatory note.

- Celebrate the success of friends and family. Take them out to dinner, bake cookies or a cake, send flowers to their office, write a personal congratulatory card, or shout out their achievements on your social media.

Chapter Eleven

Dog is My Zen...Take Time to Unwind

-11-

There is no other dog who delights in "chilling out" or taking time to unwind more than little Henry. Often mistaken for a Cavalier King Charles Spaniel, my little

Japanese Chin is the master of Zen. Maybe it's his "Asian origin" or his cat-like character that make him appear completely unfazed and unimpressed by anything. Most of his day is spent seeking out places where he can stretch out his little body and soak up a little restful relaxation.

Prior to bringing him into our home, I really did not know much about his breed. The Japanese Chin was bred from the Pekingese and the Tibetan Spaniel. Japanese royalty desired these little companions as sleeve dogs to be kept in their kimonos. Most are under 10 pounds and quite small in size. Henry is a pretty solid 18 pounds and able to run with the big dogs without any problem: earning him the moniker "Double Chin." We later learned that the larger version of this breed is referred to as an Imperial Chin, which accounts for his regal attitude and aloof "cat-like" behavior.

Henry is the most comical dog I have ever met and, while incredibly well trained, he explores each day on his own terms. He loves to go to work, strutting inside with his tail twittering and delights in gracing everyone with his presence. He looks up with a face that resembles a gremlin and waits for positive acknowledgement that he has arrived. If you are lucky, he allows you to pet him; if not, you'll get a little tail wag before he does an about face to start his day. After making his morning rounds, he seeks out the perfect location just outside our warehouse to soak up the sunshine and spend some quiet time away from his rambunctious counterpart, BOLO. He lays in the middle of the parking lot, stretched out for hours, coming to life only when he hears the rumble of the UPS truck heading in his direction. The noise showcases classical conditioning at its finest. Henry knows inside the truck is a man wearing brown who always delivers treats. Henry's reaction is reminiscent of childhood days of hearing the unique musical sounds from down the street and racing out in time to get ice cream before the truck moved along.

I wish I had the ability to take some time to unwind and put a little Zen in my life. There is no denying that I desperately need to embrace yoga or practice meditation but, for reasons I can't explain, I find it almost impossible to allow myself to slow down even for a minute. Trying to put that level of mindful calm into my brain actually creates stress for me. From the moment my feet hit the ground at 4:15 am until the time I go to sleep at around 10pm, every single minute is filled with something.

On any given day of the year, I pack 18 hours worth of activity into a 12-hour period. Believe me, this is not something I share with pride. It has been who I am for as long as I can remember. My brain is going a mile a minute most days, and no sooner do I complete one task than it's on to another. On the rare occasion I sit down to watch TV, I find myself challenged to just sit there and watch. I can maximize use of the time by reading a magazine or my latest book, following up on email, or simply fold the laundry. I drive my family nuts going from one thing to the next seamlessly without a single second to spare. I truly struggle to find a way to step back and just breathe. Of all the doggie inspirations, "Make Time for Play" and "Take Time to Unwind" will certainly be the most difficult for me to master.

I have acknowledged that it is not humanly possible to maintain the manic pace I currently run on for the remainder of my life. Quite frankly, I want to use my energy more constructively. Finding some way to access my Zen and actually take time to unwind is critical if I am to bring a sense of peaceful calm to my life. I recently had the opportunity to take steps in the right direction.

Following a weekend business retreat, I was gifted a wonderful opportunity for a spa day. My scheduled appointment was for 10am, and I needed to arrive 15 minutes early. Up since 3am, I had already caught up on email and hit the gym for my daily workout. One last thing I needed to check off my to-do list before I could head off to the spa was a training call with a new sales rep group. The call ended just minutes before I was supposed to check in at the hotel spa. I flew out the door, bolting toward the elevator and feeling my heart racing out of fear of arriving late.

I burst through the doors to this calm oasis like a tornado. The aromatherapy permeated the foyer as soft music played calmly. The young ladies behind the counter were quiet, calm, and smiled as they spoke very softly reminding me that I should have arrived 10 minutes prior for my check-in process. The look on my face as I profusely apologized made them a little more empathetic, and they suddenly seemed to sense my deep need for the services that would be rendered over the next few hours. I wondered if they were secretly aware that my mind and body had gone from zero to 60miles per hour from the moment my feet hit the floor earlier in the morning.

After changing into my fluffy soft robe, I took a few deep breaths and tried to appear peaceful as my aesthetician led me to the first treatment room to get a facial. Before she started to explain how my time at the spa would be spent, I did a quick calculation on the time change between where I was on the east coast and what it was at home on the west coast. I found relief in knowing that on the west coast it was still a couple hours before I would normally be at work. “Ugh, unbelievable!” I thought. “I am rationalizing that it’s okay for me to take this time to myself because technically it’s before my normal working hours.” The aesthetician asked me to breathe in deeply. I felt certain she could see right through my facade and knew I was wired. The aroma she placed under my nose began to calm my mind, and as she saw my body relax, she started the facial treatment.

As she cleansed and massaged my face, the thoughts racing through my mind gave new definition to the phrase “utterly ridiculous.” The conversation in my head went something like this, Ahhh, relaxation at last. Great! Oh, I need to get pricing on products for a proposal, and oh yeah, I also need to send off the spreadsheet I did earlier. I don’t think I actually hit ‘send.’ Hey wait, stop it, you are supposed to be relaxing. C’mon, you can relax.

This feels nice. I'm tired, maybe I can go to sleep—good, just breathe. Don't forget to send out follow-up emails to all the people you met at the conference, and later you can start the weekly blog. Stop it—go to sleep."

The facial lasted 45 minutes, and for 30 minutes of it, my brain would not turn off. Just as I was about to succumb completely to the peaceful sounds and scents in the room, the facial ended. I enjoyed the weak-in-the-knees feeling as I stood up to get back into my warm fluffy robe and willingly followed the spa hostess to the steam room. I was tired and eager to feel the heat and to sweat out a little stress and extra water retention. I was happy when I realized that the only thing I was focused on was the sweat that was starting to bead up all over my body. I sat there sweating for 20 minutes and became thankful that I could be alone with myself and not have thoughts racing through my head. The knock on the door brought me back to full consciousness, and I toweled up to move to the next room where a warm aromatherapy bubble bath awaited me.

As I slid into the bubbles, my mind surrendered completely and, for the first time since I can remember, I felt the real sense of relaxation and, dare I say, serenity. Unfortunately, just as I was about to fall deeper into this state of mind, the spa hostess came to get me. Now intoxicated by the soothing music and scent of the spa, I was directed to sit in the waiting area until the massage therapist came to get me. I sat down and looked over to find another woman dressed in the same fluffy robe. She was hunched over with cell phone in hand and was frantically texting or typing some email. She looked slightly frazzled as she hurriedly worked to send out whatever information she needed to send. Sitting on the table between us was a small sign that read "No Cell Phones Please." She avoided looking at it as she typed like mad, getting her fingers to move as quickly as they could in hopes of not "getting caught." I felt like I was looking in a mirror. Almost 90 minutes prior that would have surely been me. It occurred to me that I am definitely not the only one who is challenged to relax.

Running on empty guarantees burnout and is the quickest way to destroy quality of life. Shocking! Yet so many people seem to drive themselves into the ground willingly, fully aware that the pace is unsustainable. Why? At what point in our society did this become so commonplace? What enables some to be more mindful and find ease in living in the moment, while others slow down only long enough to take a bite of their lunch in between checking their email on their computers, tweeting, and posting images on Instagram on their smart phones?

With all this in mind, I realized that living in the moment is a choice. Everything is a choice. If I would just allow myself to embrace this fact, I know I would find some serenity. Home alone for a long holiday weekend, I decided to take "time to unwind" into my own hands.

I am embarrassed to admit that I almost forgot what it is like to play and unwind, but fortunately, a holiday weekend would help me find the perfect recipe to put a little bliss back into my life. If you take two dogs to one of the best dog beaches in the country; mix with lots of sunshine, tennis balls, and surf; top it off with a holiday weekend, and throw in a mindset committed to experiencing rest and relaxation, you are guaranteed to rediscover both mindfulness and what it is like to have fun.

At the start of the holiday weekend, I dropped Jon and Abby off at the airport for a trip back east to visit family. Given that I had just spent the previous two weeks traveling first to Miami, then to Dallas, and have a few more business trips lined up in the near future, I was looking forward to some quiet time at home alone with the pups. It's always hard for Jon to leave the dogs (not so much for Abby), so I brought them with me on the drive to the airport.

The weather was perfect with a crystal blue sky, bright sun, and warm gentle winds blowing off the coastline. As I drove from the airport back to the office, BOLO looked longingly out the front window, as if detecting Huntington Beach was only about 10 minutes away. I looked at her in my rear view mirror and then said, "BOLO, you are right. We need to go to the beach!" I took the next exit and then switched my radio from the permanently fixed standard news channel to a station on Sirius XM that only played music from the 90's. I cranked up those tunes and turned the air off in the car so I could roll down the windows a bit. As the fresh air started pouring in, my smile grew from watching BOLO's ears as they flapped back while she put her nose up to the crack in the back window. Oh yeah, she knew where we were going. Henry did, too.

I loved how they came alive in anticipation of some afternoon fun. As the music blared, I reminisced about the numerous times in my 20's that I had driven to the beaches along the east cost with a carload of girlfriends. Those memories were priceless, certainly not for the faint at heart—yes, believe it or not, I was once wild, crazy, and carefree.

As I pulled up to Dog Beach and into the parking lot (where it is almost impossible to find a parking space without waiting), a car was just pulling out. Perfect! I knew this afternoon was going to be fantastic. Parked, meter filled, dogs on leash, tennis balls, poop bags, sunglasses and sunscreen: Now, we were ready to go. The walk from the car to the beach is very short, but BOLO was taunted by countless ground squirrels along the way. I struggled to keep her from racing toward them: a critical point since they were taunting her from the top of the cliffs. The walkway is lined with protective railings so people don't fall over the cliffs/rocks, but BOLO would surely bolt underneath to get to those pesky rodents. It was all I could do to keep her focused on her ball and away from the walkway.

At last, down at the beach. As usual, the dogs were required to sit and stay before leashes would come off and then it was "freedom" for us all. It was warm outside so the dogs immediately ran to the only spot of shade, directly under the lifeguard stand. Henry is such a character. He became instant friends with the cool guy guarding the beach. What a great job, being a lifeguard on Dog Beach! BOLO took off for the water, dropped her ball, and waited patiently while I took pictures of Henry and his new buddy. The next two hours were amazing as I walked along the beach. I noted that the stress and guilt from not returning immediately back to work had started to disappear.

I threw BOLO's tennis ball into the ocean over and over again. I reveled in the absolute blast she was having jumping over the waves to retrieve it and then cracked up as she discovered body surfing was a cool way to get back to shore. Henry trotted along, too, stopping to either dig into the sand periodically or just stand to enjoy the wind in his face. I found it amazing how my time at the beach with the two dogs had shifted my mental mindset so drastically and so quickly. Throughout the rest of the 4th of July weekend, we made several trips back to the beach. Countless others had the same idea. It was absolutely packed with people and their dogs. We spent an entire afternoon playing and meeting new people and their dogs Henry continued to make himself at home on different people's blankets, under the shade of various umbrellas, or sun bathing with strangers on the beach. BOLO entertained beach-goers as she played non-stop in the ocean and mastered her skills at body surfing. She even had me in the water, something I have not done in years out of fear of sharks.

Zen masters know the power of mindfulness. They know how to live in the moment, truly be present, and take time to unwind. I am so grateful for my dogs and the timing of the holiday weekend to keep me out of my office. Playing with Henry and BOLO, getting out to the beach, and getting a little sun-kissed tan was exactly what I needed. I even went out with friends and to a 4th of July party. I can honestly say that, for the first time in a long time, I embraced the idea of "taking time to unwind." I am going to make this a new habit. Thank goodness for my doggies who will make sure I don't break it!

"Don't underestimate the value of doing nothing, of just going along, listening to all the things you can't hear, and not bothering."

~ Pooch's Little Instruction Book

- Taking time to unwind is as necessary to life as breathing air. While many people feel guilty taking time for themselves, it is actually selfish not to take time to unwind. By not giving yourself the opportunity to relax, have fun, and unplug from daily stressors, the inevitable burnout negatively impacts your health, your productivity, your creativity, and the relationships you have with family and friends.

- It is a simple lesson—why waste any energy on anything else but what is occurring in the moment? Dogs don't think about anything that has occurred in the previous ten minutes and are most definitely not fretting over what MIGHT happen tomorrow. They live now, relax now, play now, and take time to unwind.

- The quickest way to speed up aging is to worry about everything and never stop to relax. It is just plain unhealthy. Take 15 minutes each day to push away from your work and step outside to enjoy the simple pleasure of breathing fresh air. Start slow by scheduling one hour of uninterrupted time to do something that helps you relax and brings a sense of peace and calm into your day.

Chapter Twelve

Make Every Day Extraordinary

-12-

make every day extraordinary.

BOLO had been in my care for only a few weeks when I began to notice a wonderful pattern developing each morning. As soon as I would wake up (typically at the crack of dawn) and go toward her crate, she would beam with excitement. Her little tail would start wagging back and forth, almost knocking herself over. I don't think I have ever seen a tail wag so fervently on any dog before. Hardly able to contain herself, she would eagerly offer up the SIT required for me to open up her crate to let her out. Since we were in "house-training" mode, she would immediately follow me downstairs and head outside to her "potty spot." After relieving herself, she would return to me, tripping over her puppy feet and wagging her entire body, falling all over me as I sat on the stairs to greet her good morning.

Day after day would start off this way and, as she grew, she became increasingly more excited to start a new day. In fact, she was so excited to start her day that it forced me to stop and take notice. As I sat on the edge of my bed thinking about my other dogs, it occurred to me that none of them ever woke up like BOLO. The moment BOLO's eyes opened, her tail would start to thump loudly and wag like crazy. Her body would follow suit, indicating that she was about to explode with excitement. Once her crate door opened, she would grab her Kong and move about with so much enthusiasm and joy as if to say, "Hooray! It's a new day! OMG, can you believe it? I am so excited to start another day! I can't wait to do all the things I get to do, explore places, go for my walk, hang out with my family, etc!"

Now as a two year old, 63-pound, fully house-trained dog, she no longer needs to race outside first thing in the morning. Having graduated from her crate to our bed, she waits patiently for me to open my eyes. Although I can't see her with my eyes closed, I feel her staring at me as I come out of my night's slumber. I imagine she is thinking to herself, "Hurry up, wake up, we are missing valuable time in our day already!" My eyes part slowly in a very tight squinting position so I can get a peek at what she is doing before the mayhem begins. Sure enough, her eyes locked solidly on me, she comes to life instantly. Her eyes widen, and her mouth takes on a doggie smile. If she had hands, this would be the moment she would clap them together and yell out, "Yea! Game on! Let's get this party started!" This is the moment when she leaps off the bed to find the nearest toy and then pummels me with her crazy morning greeting. I am pinned in my bed as she steps over me, going back and forth while her body wags wildly out of control. In her excitement, she trips over me, steps on me, and repeatedly tries to push her toy into my mouth over and over again before she finally buries her head in my neck while leaving her wagging tail in the air. She will finally collapse on me, panting and is simply thrilled to be experiencing everything about this morning rise-and-shine ritual. When I am able to finally break free from the love fest, she follows me with toy in mouth and never once stops wagging her entire body. You can see the happiness emanating from her eyes.

She is always so darn elated every single morning that I wondered, "What would my days be like if I woke up like this everyday? I think they would be phenomenal!"

"Each morning we are born again. What we do today is what matters most."

~ Buddha

I don't mind getting out of bed in the morning. In fact I love to get up each day, especially before dawn. In the past year though, as much as I love getting up early, I can honestly say I was not jumping out of bed with emotional enthusiasm. Despite the fact that I have a successful and growing business to go to each day and amazing people that I get to work with, I just did not feel a pure intrinsic sense of joy to take on the day. Looking at BOLO's angelic eyes beaming with life and watching how she greeted each day made me stop and think, "Hey, everyday is an extraordinary gift, and it is my moral obligation to be happy and set my mindset to make each experience in the day extraordinary."

Moral obligation? Really, you might ask? That was my initial thought when I first heard this from radio talk show host, Dennis Prager. As I came to understand his philosophy behind the statement, it made perfect sense. It is incredibly unfair to impose unhappiness and negativity on others around you. Think about how an unhappy parent affects the development of a child, how an unhappy spouse affects a marriage, and how an unhappy employee affects morale at work. I could go on, but I'm sure you get the point.

Unhappy people exude negativity through their moodiness, reactivity, and constant complaining. The unintended consequences of not making a point to be happy and create extraordinary experiences during each day can leave lasting scars on relationships with family members, friendships, or co-workers. Despite creating carnage through the drama they inflict on others, unhappy people find reinforcement in the attention they receive from those around them. Sure, family tolerates our lack of filter and self-control, and friends willingly allow us to vent to them, but as you can imagine, they can't possibly feel good in those moments or be able to maintain heightened levels of their own happiness. With all this in mind, it becomes more apparent why being happy or faking happiness is a moral obligation to others around us.

I've come to realize the critical importance of this simple statement. How I think, behave, and react has a direct effect on how others experience their days. One's mood directly impacts the tone of your voice, the sharpness or softness of your tongue, your body language, and how you interact with others. It's incredibly unfair to impose anger, constant frustration, and unhappiness on others.

So it really is a moral obligation to get your own happiness in check. Because "stuff" happens, and it's human nature to react or shift on a dime depending on what's going on around us, how do you maintain a happy demeanor and do it consistently?

For me, it started with a decision. Guess what? Every day when you wake up, you can actually lie there for a second and decide in an instant what kind of day it is going to be.

It actually is that simple—it starts with the decision as to how you will live in this new day.

I was intent on turning everything around in my life. It was no longer enough just to wake up and get through the day. I wanted to LIVE the day. How could I make each day an extraordinary experience? Waking up like BOLO could change the entire day's experience.

The cliché, "Live each day as if it is your last" provokes interesting thought. Yeah, we say it, but most people don't make the decision to do it. Why? Because when your alarm goes off you either just get up and start going through your established routine, or you hit snooze to avoid having to break out of the cocoon called your bed. If you are like most people, your approach to the day is the same as it was the day before; you are on autopilot. Very few people take the time to actually design how the day will unfold. Understand that there is a difference between designing your day and creating a to-do list. To-do lists establish the objectives you will attend to during the day and help to focus your attention. They provide direction and clarity on what needs to be done in order to achieve your goals. However they don't impact HOW you will experience the day.

"It's only when we truly know and understand that we have a limited time on earth—and that we have no way of knowing when our time is up—that we will begin to live each day to the fullest, as if it was the only one we had."

~ Elisabeth Kübler-Ross

So, how do you design your day so that you experience it in a way that serves you and others? I recently attended a business conference where one of the speakers said something so simple yet so profound that it hit me like a ton of bricks.

During her presentation, she stated, "You only get one life. Once today is over, it's gone, FOREVER. You will never EVER get it back. So how are you going to be today?" Her words left me sitting there stunned. The message was not some shocking new information. I already intuitively knew you only get one chance at living your life, but it was the way she put her emphasis on the fact that once a day was gone, you NEVER get it back. I felt she was talking directly to me as if to say, "Hey, when are you going to wake up and live how you were intended to live? Why are you being so unfair to yourself by letting each day pass you by without making something about it memorable and without engaging in things you enjoy?" With my 50th birthday just around the corner, I suddenly feared growing old and looking back on my life with regret. That was too painful a thought to entertain.

And so I sat there, thinking about how I wanted to be and how I was going to be. Asking the question, "How are you going to be?" vs. "What are you going to do today?" shifted my mentality. I did not want to run through my checklist of things to do and call it a day. I was ready to put the brakes on living each day by default and take a proactive approach in determining how the day would unfold. I made a decision to choose how I would feel, how

I would interact with others, to notice things around me, and to take time to review all that I had to be grateful for. To some, this may initially seem like an insurmountable task, but there is one thing about my personality that I know with unbridled certainty: I am disciplined.

To effectively design my day, I had to shift how the entire day began, beginning with answering the question that the speaker had presented to the audience. "How will I be today?" I wrote out the question on a 4X6 file card and just answered it. In fact, every day since this conference, I write out this question and answer it. On most days, the answers to the question are the same. On others, I add something else more specific based on the to-do list for the day. I took time to determine how I would be toward people and how I would respond to things occurring during my day when they did not go as expected. I would decide upon something kind and thoughtful I could do for someone. The bottom line was that I was going to choose to be happy, be good to myself and others, stay focused on things that were important, maintain a level of patience and calm, stay energetic yet pace myself, notice the gifts of nature in the world around me, stop to be grateful for all the wonderful things in my life, and to smile at everyone.

Smiling at everyone would be the one thing that truly set the tone for the day. This was an interesting experiment. I always smile at people I know or people who are serving me in some way (a waiter/waitress, bank teller, the checker at the grocery store, etc.), but now I was going to look directly at everyone I encountered and smile. It felt weird at first, but I was curious as to how people would respond. To help produce a smile naturally, I would just think of something that made me laugh (usually thoughts of the crazy dog antics I see every day). What I discovered was that every single person I smiled at, smiled back. When they smiled back, it made me smile more.

Every day when I leave my house, I remind myself to smile at everyone. I do this now when I am in the car, a store, a restaurant, the gas station, the gym, etc... The most entertaining place to do this though is in the airport. What I discovered was that smiling at someone in the airport caused them to turn their heads to see who I was looking at. Because I was a stranger, these people assumed my smile could not possibly be intended for them. However they often turned back and reciprocated. Interestingly, after a couple months of practice, this new personal initiative has become a habit, and not once has the recipient of my smile ever turned away and not returned the gesture.

Let me be clear that, although I intentionally think through how I will be each day, not every day is like roses and honey for me. Deciding up front what your state of mind will be throughout the day and then following through completely boils down to one's ability to control emotional responses. This is not an easy task. Like exercising any other muscle, dedicated daily attention is required in order to strengthen positive responses. What this practice does for me, however, is remind me that at any given moment, I can choose to be a certain way. Becoming more cognizant of the thoughts or behaviors that are not serving me well, I can take a second to think about how I need to be in order to make my day a good experience.

"One can make a day of any size, and regulate the rising and setting of his own sun and the brightness of its shining."

~John Muir

- Decide within the first 10 minutes of waking up exactly what type of energy you will bring to the day. Write it down on paper or a file card, and refer to it throughout the day to keep yourself on track.

- Predetermine your response to unexpected things that get thrown your way. Learn how to take a breath before reacting. Avoid explosive angry responses, which will negatively affect the people around you and make it more difficult to experience the remainder of the day positively. Set the stage for how you will react to things that come your way, decide what you will do to positively impact others, and make a decision on the type of energy you will bring to the day.

- Do something special for others. Look for ways to engage in random acts of kindness. Bring co-workers bagels or donuts in the morning, or buy coffee for the person in line behind you. This "pay it forward" approach makes the day more memorable and elevates your mood as well.

Find ways to break up your routine and try something new in order to experience the day differently. Skip the gym in lieu of a morning hike, try a new place to pick up your coffee, take a friend out to lunch and try something new on the menu, or take a different route home from work.

Chapter Thirteen

A Dog Can Change the Way You See the World

-13-

a dog
can change
the way
you see
the world.

Perfection is a perception. Dogs will quickly make you fully aware that perfection is fantasy.

BOLO came into my life as an idea in January of 2013 during a tradeshow, where I met the Director of Philanthropic Giving for Leader Dogs for the Blind. During our conversation, it became immediately evident that this man was incredibly passionate about the mission behind Leader Dogs. The organization, based in Rochester Hills, Michigan, has been serving the blind, visually impaired, and deaf since the1930's. As I learned about their program, he shared ways in which other companies supported their cause. Some companies donated money for the right to name a puppy, highlight its progress throughout the first year, and promote the Leader Dog program. Others actually had staff members raise a puppy for a year.

I was absolutely fascinated! Immediately my mind started spinning with ideas. Of course, given the fact that my mantra is, "If it's worth doing, it's worth overdoing," visions of becoming an official puppy raiser and designing a year-long fundraising and awareness campaign started racing through my head. Because I am a professional dog trainer, my initial thought was that this would be super easy. I fell in love with the idea of doing something bigger than myself and was motivated to launch a fundraising campaign much greater than we had ever done before as a company. After selling Jon on the idea and assuring him this was not something I would jump into the moment I returned from the tradeshow, "The BOLO Project" was born.

My brain vacillated between the excitement for the potential of this project and thoughts of my sweet Sasha who was recovering at home following the amputation of her back leg. A few weeks prior, cancer was detected, and the vet recommended amputation because of the severe pain it was causing her. She was 12 years old at the time, and we made this decision based on the fact that she was otherwise perfectly healthy, happy, and would be able to enjoy a good quality of life. Plus I could not bear to watch her in pain.

With Sasha's recovery on my mind, I knew I could not embark on such an elaborate project that involved bringing a young puppy into my home. Six months later, in June of 2013, we had to say goodbye to our girl. Many of you have experienced the heart-wrenching final moments in a vet's office with your dog lying in your lap. The tears flowed uncontrollably as we watched Sasha's eyes close slowly and her last breath left her body. She crossed peacefully over "Rainbow Bridge".

Shortly after Sasha passed away, Leader Dogs contacted me to let me know a litter of new puppies would be born in August. They wanted to know if I was willing to start the process after BOLO's arrival. This would give me time to grieve for Sasha and prepare for the idea of a new puppy in the house.

BOLO was born August 2, 2013. The next day, we received a generous gift from the Director of Philanthropic Giving. Maybe he secretly knew about my weakness for frosting because delivered to our headquarters, fresh from Sprinkles, were a dozen of the most beautiful and delicious cupcakes announcing BOLO's arrival in the world. Seven weeks later, September 15th, I boarded a flight for Michigan to pick up this canine gift to the world.

You can imagine my squeals the moment I got to lay eyes on BOLO. There she was in the puppy area with some of her littermates. She was the only puppy with a tail that wagged back and forth at top speed. While others were playing with each other, she was happy to look out beyond the playpen at the people and shook her little body and wagged that tail nonstop. Even now, as I type up these memories, a huge smile forms on my face.

I was ready to pour everything I had into BOLO's care and training and eagerly soaked up the information and training provided to all the puppy raisers. I just knew it was going to be a perfect year. Amidst all the excitement, I thought about how I was going to add raising a perfect puppy and run a perfect marketing/fundraising campaign to my growing list of daily responsibilities.

I am a perfectionist and—while I did not overtly voice my thoughts—anything less than perfection in the training, the project, the marketing, and the product line was not an option.

I would soon discover that juggling all of these things along with my existing obligations to generate product sales for Dog is Good, create the product concept for the line that would support The BOLO Project, coordinate with team members on the implementation of marketing, manage the warehouse and small staff, be a good mom and supportive wife, follow through with my volunteer obligations, AND train the puppy (publicly) would become a bit overwhelming. Perfection was no longer an option, despite my efforts to fight it every step of the way.

The weekend in Michigan went by quickly and before I knew it I had BOLO in my arms. Ahhh, I swear there is nothing better than puppy's breath. The moment her little snout made contact with my nose, I took in a full whiff of this intoxicating aroma. It sounds crazy, but puppy people know exactly what I am talking about. She relaxed in my arms as I thanked the puppy development team for putting their faith and trust in me to raise a well-mannered, behaviorally sound puppy for their program. Then off we went, to return to California.

All was good until my dear friend and I got into the car to drive to the airport. I had put BOLO in a travel crate to keep her safe, and as we got underway, the most horrible shrill began to emanate from it. It was so bad that we had to pull over to see if something was seriously wrong. While I knew a lot about raising puppies, I felt nervous about this one. She had been entrusted in my care and did not really belong to me. What could possibly be causing this puppy to cry so loudly? After we pulled over, I took her out of her crate. There was nothing wrong, but I could not suppress my momma instinct, so I held this sweet pup for a few minutes, rocking her to sleep before putting her back in her crate so we could get underway.

It's an interesting thing to see what happens when you are holding a seven-week-old Yellow Lab puppy. At the airport and safely through security, out she came from her carrier. Like bees to honey, people started to flock over to touch her. If they did not physically come over, they looked our way with a smile and expression of joy.

Surprisingly there were even people trying to walk backwards on the moving sidewalk to get their puppy fix. I began to refer to this phenomenon as "BOLO-mania." The obvious symptoms included glazing over of the eyes, open mouth squealing, the flapping of excitable hands, and overt oooohs and aaaahs combined with begging to pet this oh-so-irresistible pup. It amazed me how she changed the demeanor of everyone.

Throughout the entire year she was in my care, the phenomenon continued. What fascinated me was the extent to which people's excitement elevated, and how I literally could not walk two or three feet in a public location without getting stopped. Whenever we were out and about, people halted in their tracks then walked immediately in our direction. People changed the moment they laid eyes on her.

One evening out, a woman stunned both my family and her dinner date when she became so fixated on BOLO that she nearly leapt over a banister separating the restaurant patio from the walkway where we were standing. On a separate occasion at a restaurant, one poor guy patiently waited while his girlfriend fawned all over BOLO and then became exasperated when the waitress joined in the love fest. He threw his arms up saying, "Great! This puppy is getting more attention than I ever have, and now I can't even order a beer!" Even my 26-year-old (single) nephew wanted to get in on a little BOLO-mania, asking if he could "watch" her for the day down in Newport Beach. I suppose it's understandable that my handsome, single nephew would ask to "borrow" BOLO while spending time near the beach, but who was he kidding? I knew the ulterior motive, and there was no way I was going to allow BOLO to be his "chick magnet."

My disciplined approach to training helped structure BOLO's environment and daily routine. Many families who hire my dog training services, discover that their dogs end up "training" them. They become responsive "trainees" reacting to their dog's behavior and inadvertently reinforce the very behaviors they hope to eliminate. Fully aware of this, I made sure I was the trainer for BOLO at all times and was always on task at home, at work, in a grocery store, downtown, in a mall, etc. She was such a cheerful and easy puppy and willingly followed my lead. Housetraining—an urgent and critically important task to accomplish for any dog in a home—was mastered quickly.

She happily went along with everything, learning at max speed, and I was pleased with how "perfect" she was becoming. My need to ensure she was perfect made it impossible for anyone else to work with her. In hindsight, there were numerous times when I needed a break or a chance to focus on something else. It would have been helpful to have others walk her or do some basic training, but I was so concerned about her ability to pass the testing that I just could not relinquish any control over training. Later, I would realize that this obsessive concern was more about me and my desire for perfection.

I had internalized her training and performance as a reflection on me as a person and as a trainer. I feared failure and doing anything less than producing the next amazing guide dog. With each passing month, the self-imposed pressure grew stronger. Everyone around me was completely unaware of the pending implosion that was building up inside as I kept a smile on my face at all times and exuded the appearance of someone who could easily go by the moniker of "Wonder Woman."

Then one day it happened. BOLO was five months old and, as we were walking down Main Street in Seal Beach, she suddenly seemed to forget everything I had been teaching her since day one. Now, for any puppy at this age, this is normal. But BOLO was not just any puppy. On this particular day, I had a lot lined up on the to-do list. I needed to get through this training walk in public so I could get to work and get stuff done. BOLO had other ideas. She wanted to explore and was not at all interested in staying by my side and stopping at every corner. Suddenly, she was pulling me to wherever she wanted to go, she would not stay for her "sit-stay," she would not lay down on command, and she tried to eat every little thing on the ground that caught her eye. My to-do list was scrolling through my head like a ticker tape, causing my patience to quickly turn to exasperation.

In the meantime, as I was trying to deal with this rambunctious puppy, a friend called. She needed to talk to me about some challenges she was going through. I tried to listen, but my attention was really not on her at all, and

I was challenged to respond to what she was saying. Regretfully, I was a little abrupt before I said I had my hands full with an out-of-control puppy and could not simultaneously deal with the puppy and talk on the phone.

BOLO was just being a puppy, enjoying the world around her, but I needed her to be a Leader Dog in training. All I could think about was that I was failing in the moment. We walked a few feet further when I suddenly teared up at having ended my conversation with my friend because I simply could not let BOLO do anything but what she was supposed to be doing. I let my friend down, I let BOLO down, and I had let myself down. I got to a place where I could not be seen and just started to cry. The fragile glass that had formed around my world already had many cracks. In this moment, a new crack developed. Like the straw that broke the camel's back, this new crevice would weaken the structure so much that it would be impossible for it to stand anymore, and it shattered instantly. The crashing of this glass wall, covered with fissures produced over 40+ years, came down hard...so hard it frightened me.

In the ensuing months, I would try to maintain my ability to perform anything with peak performance. Inside I was dying and when alone would cry uncontrollably for hours. I became anxious, withdrawn, lost weight, and discovered that all my old coping mechanisms were challenged to work effectively for me.

The next six months would prove to be very difficult. It took everything I had to employ my acting skills so that outwardly, with the exception of becoming painfully thin, most people had no idea that anguish and depression had seriously consumed my soul. I struggled to employ the one coping mechanism that had always served me well—burying myself in my work. I continued to focus heavily on preparing BOLO for success. All the self-imposed pressure made it impossible for me to be present in anything I was doing. When I was training, I felt guilty and worried that I was not generating sales; when BOLO distracted me while I was trying to work with accounts and bring in new business, I felt guilty that I was not focused on her. It was a vicious cycle and, through it all, I never made time for fun or do anything that would bring me intrinsic joy.

As the year with BOLO started to wind down, I now had a new issue to address... the reality that I would soon be letting her go. I wondered how so many others handled the process of returning future Leader Dog puppies after getting so attached, falling in love, and bonding. The last few months were filled with mixed emotions. On the one hand, both Jon and I welcomed a little reprieve and the chance to put a bit of normalcy back into our lives. With "The BOLO Project" complete, maybe it was possible to begin pulling myself up from the depths to which I had spiraled.

The last two months with BOLO went by quickly. It was now time to take this well socialized and trained year-old puppy back to Leader Dogs for the Blind where she would enter the next phase of her training. By this point, I had come to terms with the original objective of our mission—to be a force for good and do something that would truly impact another person's life. I embraced the idea that letting her go was not about what I was giving up; it was about what I was giving.

Once again I boarded a plane for Michigan. My friend joined me on the journey, which would have been too hard for me to do alone. My fears covered the gamut from the emptiness that would fill my home to the worries of how she would do on her initial behavioral and obedience test. The Perfectionist was rearing her ugly head again. To my delight, BOLO scored beautifully on the required obedience skills. The folks at Leader Dogs for the Blind were very happy with how she had grown and how well mannered she had become. They were kind and understanding and knew the emotional challenge I was facing, like many others before me, upon returning her to the facility. After a tearful good-bye, I went to visit with the man who gave me this wonderful opportunity to make a difference. Rather than ask me about BOLO or how I was feeling, he proceeded to share stories of the people fortunate enough to have received one of the Leader Dogs. I sat quietly listening and, by the time I had left his office, I felt a renewed sense of accomplishment knowing that my year with BOLO would literally change someone's life. I did not, for one minute, think that life would be *mine*.

Seven weeks had passed, and we were all adjusting to life without BOLO. Sitting in a staff meeting, my phone rang. It was Leader Dogs for the Blind and, fearing something was wrong, I answered the call. They informed me that she just did not want to come out of her kennel and did not want to "work" so they made the decision to have her make a "career change." They wanted to know if I would be willing to take her back as a pet dog (For a variety of reasons, only about 50% of the puppies make it all the way through the program.). Everyone in the conference room was elated. I was stunned. I couldn't talk. I mustered up enough voice to tell them, "Yes, of course, I will take her back." A lump in my throat formed as the voice in my head kept telling me, "You failed. You failed BOLO, you failed Leader Dogs, you failed the person she would serve. You simply failed."

BOLO's destiny was to be a guide dog for someone visually impaired. In a way, this still holds true. She came back to a person (me) whose vision of herself and the role she played in the world were deeply impaired.

She had been back in our care for only a few weeks when I experienced something special. One morning, after letting BOLO out of her crate, I sat on my bed just watching her. I watched as she tripped over her puppy feet while her body engaged in a full body wag. She could not wait to greet Henry and Jon. The pure happiness that was generating from her entire body permeated the room. For the first time in months, I felt a natural smile come to my face. I felt this peculiar feeling that I had not felt in so long—happiness. I loved how I felt in that moment and wanted more of it. I watched her play, and when I got down on the floor to sit with her, she could hardly contain herself.

From that moment forward, as I spent time with this still-growing puppy, I began to re-evaluate my personality and the choices I made to get me where I am today. With the pressure of training her publicly off my plate, I began to look at BOLO differently. I started to notice how she behaved and reacted to things. Despite years as a dog trainer, used to observing animal behavior, I changed the channel from which I was viewing. The new perspective would be life changing for me. I loved how she moved, how she took on each day, how she explored her world, greeted others, played full tilt, and brought joy to everyone she encountered. I began to embrace the idea of taking cues from the behavior of dogs, in other words, live a life inspired by Dog. My hope was that, in doing so, I might discover a sense of peace and true happiness, which seemed to evade me for so long.

BOLO came into this world to be the "eyes" and provide independence for someone visually impaired. Instead, she has given me the chance to look at my world through new lenses: providing me with renewed vision, hope, the chance to learn and grow, re-discover my life's purpose, take responsibility for my own happiness, and create success as I define it.

A dog truly can change how you see the world. If you are open to looking at life through the eyes of a dog, it can create a shift in how you live, how you forge rewarding relationships, how you approach your work or growing business, and give you strength to face the fears that prevent you from living your ideal life.

"When you change the way you look at things, the things you look at change."

~ Dr. Wayne Dwyer

- Stop and spend time with a puppy whenever you can. Take in everything wonderful about the puppy: how it looks, how it feels, how it smells, and the smile and pure joy it brings to your heart. I can promise the experience will elevate any mood.

- Embrace the fact that perfection is a myth. Holding onto this unrealistic idea means you will never "win." It paralyzes progress and will literally destroy the essence of your soul.

- Understand that no one is really watching you. In fact, most people are so caught up in their own personal worlds that they really have very little time to focus on what is going right or wrong in yours, we are our own worst critics. The self-inflicted attacks will kill any natural joy.

Are You Inspired by Dog? Submit Your Story!

It was my intense love of dogs and awareness of the positive benefits dogs have on our lives that led me to co-found Dog is Good. The success of the brand lies in our messaging and its ability to elicit an immediate emotional response from dog lovers. Because so many of us share a love of dogs and find inspiration and contentment in their company,

Dog is Good has been able to connect with dog lovers worldwide. Celebrating the relationship between humans and dogs, the Dog is Good brand uses humor, sentiment, real-life observation and sophisticated design to create artwork and products that dog lovers immediately relate to. The company sells online, into retail stores in the US and several other countries, and licenses the brand to numerous manufacturers As the company continues to focus on life inspired by Dog, they are expanding to include services and membership opportunities.

The dogs who have touched my heart—Zoe, Sasha, Henry, BOLO—and the hundreds I have trained over the years have profoundly impacted my life. I know that I am not unique in my experiences, so I invite you to submit your personal stories on lessons you have learned from your own dog(s). Your photos and stories will be shared on the Dog is Good website as inspiration to others.

To submit stories about your life with Dog—whether poignant or humorous—go to:

www.dogisgood.com/come-dig-with-us/me-my-dog

You may also submit a tribute to your dog(s) to celebrate the memories and joys created during your time with them. Go to: www.dogisgood.com/tribute

Contact us at:

info@dogisgood.com
10531 Humbolt Street
Los Alamitos, CA 90720

About the Author

Gila grew up in Northern Virginia and attended Virginia Tech University where she graduated with a degree in Secondary Education in 1987. Her teaching career began in a suburb of Baltimore, MD immediately thereafter. It was to be a short-lived career because she soon attended a bid-for-bachelors fundraiser auction where, with her VISA card, she purchased her future husband. His naval career was not particularly compatible with her teaching career, and the latter effectively ended when they married in 1989 and proceeded to move about every two or three years. In 2006, they moved to their final Navy duty station in Seal Beach, CA, and stayed there afterward to give their daughter some geographic stability, to build the Dog is Good business, and because the weather is perfect.

Over the years, in addition to supporting a stressful navy lifestyle, Gila always had some sort of sales gig going on. After she convinced Jon that they needed to adopt a Dalmatian puppy, Gila learned she really liked dogs and decided to pursue a career as a dog trainer. She immersed herself in the study and application of the science of canine behavior and quickly became the go-to dog trainer wherever she moved (much to the disappointment of the third human Kurtz family member, daughter Abby).

The Dog is Good business evolved slowly from an idea in 2005 to a part-time business in 2007, to a full-fledged operation in a small warehouse in 2009. Dog is Good is now a nationally recognized brand, renowned for clever and poignant messaging that resonates with dog lovers. The business has won numerous awards in both the pet and gift industries, including the coveted "Louie" award in 2011 from the Greeting Card Association. Gila has been the recipient of several business awards, including recognition as one of the top 25 Women of Influence in the Pet Industry (2015) by Pet Age. In addition to her role as VP of Sales for Dog is Good, Puppy Training Expert, and Number One Fan to daughter Abby, Gila speaks professionally on life lessons learned: inspired by dog, overcoming small business challenges, and on best practice parenting strategies to "raise your child like a dog".

Her interests include running, weight lifting, hiking, any outdoor activity, reading non-fiction, baking, watching her daughter perform on stage, and—of course—beach time with her dogs.

A recurring theme with Gila is that "Anything worth doing is worth overdoing."

Connect with Dog Is Good and the Author

Dog Is Good
10531 Humbolt Street
Los Alamitos, CA 90720

Office: 562.735.0219
FAX: 562-684-4161
gila@dogisgood.com

Web: www.dogisgood.com
Like us on **Facebook**: www.facebook.com/dogisgood
Follow us on **Linked In**:
www.linkedin.com/company/dog-is-good
See us on **Pinterest**: pinterest.com/digdogisgood
Follow us on **Twitter**: www.twitter.com/dogisgood

Online Catalog:
drive.google.com/a/dogisgood.com/file/d/0B_v4PfHk6R
otWEl3c005VmhoUUE/view

Resources

Canfield, Jack, *The Success Principles*

Maxwell, John, *15 Invaluable Laws of Growth*

Maxwell, John, *How Successful People Think*

Morrissey, Mary, *Dream Builder Live Program*

LifeHack.org

Made in the USA
San Bernardino, CA
06 February 2017